SHARED SPLENDOR

SHARED SPLENDOR

J · E · A · N · I · E
M · I · L · E · Y

Fleming H. Revell Company
Tarrytown, New York

Library of Congress Cataloging-in-Publication Data
Miley, Jeanie.
Shared splendor / Jeanie Miley.
    p.   cm.
   ISBN 0-8007-1659-0
   1. Interpersonal relations—Religious aspects—Christianity.
2. Prayer.   3. Miley, Jeanie.   I. Title.
BV4597.52.M54   1991
248.4—dc20   91-17222
                                                        CIP

Copyright © 1991 by Jeanie Miley
Published by the Fleming H. Revell Company
Tarrytown, New York 10591
Printed in the United States of America

Gratefully and lovingly dedicated to
Floyd Thatcher,
faithful friend . . . teacher
and instrument of Christ's Splendor

Acknowledgments

Throughout the writing of *Shared Splendor*, God has drawn near over and over through human instruments who have given encouragement and support in ways too numerous to count.

I am forever indebted to Nancy Slaughter and the women of the San Angelo class of Community Bible Study who have been such an important part of my life during the last two years. For the women and men who have shared their lives and experiences through the retreats, workshops, seminars, and spiritual growth groups of Growth Options, I am deeply grateful.

Howard and Carole Hovde have gently encouraged me through these years of stretching, and Madeleine L'Engle has been an invaluable source of inspiration and courage for me along the pathway to becoming a writer.

The members of Southland Baptist Church have graciously given me nurturing for my own spiritual growth. They have encouraged my freedom as a person and my diligence as a writer, and I treasure the relationship with them. In so many ways, they are family to me.

There is no way I can adequately thank those who have given practical help. Charlotte Caffey has done innumerable tasks throughout the years to facilitate my life, and she has done those tasks with unselfishness, grace, and excellence. I couldn't have made it without her help. Stan Joynton and Mike Bodiford have given more than they know in stability and practical guidance, and I appreciate them so very much.

My family has always been of utmost importance to me, but through the writing of this book, I have become acutely aware of how precious each of them is to me. The influence of each of them is on the pages of this book.

Indeed, I am supremely fortunate to live in communion and in community with these and so many others who are such gracious instruments of God's love.

Jeanie Miley
San Angelo, Texas

Contents

Introduction: A New Way of Seeing

Luke tells us about two disciples traveling toward Emmaus after the crucifixion of Christ. Lost and confused and focused on their own hopelessness and helplessness, they made their way away from Jerusalem. These two had a terrible problem.

Jesus appeared to them, walking with them on their journey, talking with them, and later sharing a meal. When He broke bread with them, *their eyes were opened*. They saw what they had not been able to see before. *In the presence of Christ, everything changed*.

That same empowering Presence comes to us now in our own confusion and fear, longing to give us love, to free us to love.

The call to love one another was a radical one in the first century. The call to be channels of Christ's love now is radical. What have we got to lose? And what have we got to gain?

Those two traveling disciples teach us an important lesson. When Christ makes His presence known, He starts by changing

11

the way we *see*. This is true in our relationships as well. When Christ brings peace to our relationships, He begins by altering the way we view our interaction with others.

So, how do you *see* your relationships?

• When you think about one of your significant relationships, do you automatically feel the joy in the friendship? Or does your mind search, like a computer, for the problems?

• Do you, in your mind's eye, visualize the things that give you pleasure or the things that give you pain?

• What do you say to yourself about people? Is your "self-talk" about people positive and accepting? Or do you, in the quietness of your own inner thoughts, call people names and cast judgment?

• Are you on the lookout for those "special" offenses, those irritating habits that others seem to do just for you? Do you store this data in your mental file cabinet for future use?

• Does what you think about people shape what happens when you are with them?

• Do your attitudes perpetuate peace and harmony or conflict and alienation?

• When you picture your loved ones, do you see them through gentle and soft eyes of love and acceptance? Or are your eyes hardened by criticism?

• Do you gravitate almost instinctively toward the faults and failures of others? Are you addicted to "negaholism," that dangerous evil of negative thinking?

• Do your expectations about others keep them from changing?

• Do you hold others to their past failures, reminding them of their patterns or watching for them to slip, or do you release them to be new creations?

• Do you have a favorite scapegoat, a special problem or person who gets the blame for your unhappiness? Is there some solitary soul who gets singled out to carry the blame for the problems of your workplace, your church, or your family?

• Is there an individual who is your special "project," a person you are working hard to "fix"? (Perhaps your greatest efforts and creativity are being spent in pointing out this person's faults, keeping tabs on when he acts the way you knew he would, and then lecturing him about what he should or should not have done!)

• How do you pray for others? Do you tell God how to change people, and what to do for them—all in "their best interest," of course?

Do any of these descriptions apply to you? Then maybe the first step toward healthy relationships is an "eye-opening." A new way of *seeing* the people around you may put you on a path of healing.

How would it change things to visualize the presence of Christ walking with you in your encounters with others? What would be different if you listened for the loving instructions of Christ in regard to your problem people, instead of telling Him what to do in your prayers? Would it be possible to pray about these people with no agenda of your own, but merely entrusting them to God's agenda? Can we trust God to work His wise ways, and change them—and change us—as *He* sees fit?

It will take a new way of seeing, a new way of thinking, a new way of praying.

13

SHARED SPLENDOR

1
Learning Peace Through Prayer

The man who prays not only discovers himself and God,
but in the same meeting he discovers who his neighbor is.
For in prayer, you not only profess that man is man and
God is God, but also, that your neighbor is your fellowman,
that is, a man alongside you.

—Henri Nouwen

By this all men will know that you are my disciples, if you
love one another.

John 13:35

"Why don't we have a Peace School?" I spouted to my husband one cold winter day.

Some of the military personnel in our town had been assigned
to the War School. I was fascinated by the idea of going to school
to learn how to make war.

"What would you have in your Peace School?" Martus teased
me. "What would your curriculum be?"

My imagination went to work over the next few days, as I drove
up and down the streets of San Angelo, delivering sometimes
squabbling siblings to various sites. I thought about his challenge
as I led the weekly spiritual growth groups of Growth Options and

listened to the conflicts in individuals' lives. How could those conflicts be turned into arenas of grace and peace? Would it be possible to learn how to bring about win-win solutions, eliminating the need for a loser?

Reading the daily newspaper, I wrestle with the war/peace issue. We humans certainly know how to make war. Even as I write this, war is escalating in the Persian Gulf. It splits me in two to write about Christ's transforming presence and to watch the horrors of war unfold day by day. My mind floods with questions. Can Christianity make a difference? Can individual Christians, committed to being instruments of Christ, change anything?

Participating deeply in a local church, I am well aware that we Christians have our struggles, too. We are capable of great closeness—and ugly division. As a lifelong member of a conflict-ridden denomination, I wonder how the world sees us. Is the biblical comment, "See how they love one another," being replaced by, "See how they fight with one another"?

Is it possible for Christians to live in peace with each other? Or is that an archaic notion born in an idealistic heart?

What is keeping our churches from being oases of acceptance rather than swamps of censure? Shouldn't the Bible foster encouragement and support instead of power struggles? Can we move past our immaturity and self-centeredness and become centers of transforming friendships, made possible by the presence of Christ among us?

Why can't we focus more on what unites us than on what fragments us? Can we possibly learn to celebrate our differences instead of making war over them?

And why can't Christian marriages be the best and most intimate? What keeps Christian families from having the best communication?

The fact is, we have not yet learned how to make peace. One method often attempted is to *fight back*. Our culture has

16

developed all sorts of high-tech ways of doing this. I listen in wonderment to reports on the effectiveness of Patriot missiles and I gawk at the "Christian Martial Arts" bumper sticker on the car ahead of me. (I chuckle to myself at the seeming dichotomy in concepts, all too aware of the popularity of courses in self-defense.)

In theory, I suppose, these are purely defensive strategies—peace through strength. But strength, once gained, is hard to keep in check. The Patriots may defend a nation by knocking incoming missiles out of action, but this allows us to launch missiles of our own, with deadly effect. The peaceful ideals of martial arts can be lost in the flicker of a hundred "action films" in which violence is glorified.

I recall the wisdom of my eighty-three-year-old father: <u>You cannot war your way to peace</u>.

Another method often used in our homes, workplaces, and churches is *keeping the peace*. We pretend that conflicts don't exist. We do not rock the boat. We spend inordinate amounts of energy holding down our real feelings and covering up the truth.

The result is not really peace, but denial. And this sort of "peace at any price" game costs us dearly, both in strained relationships and in personal tension.

Is there a better way? Corporate counselors, diplomats, and legal advisers keep studying conflict resolution, interpersonal dynamics, and negotiation strategies. They, too, seek peace—at their lofty levels. But what about us, in our marriages, with our children, at our churches, with our co-workers? How do we live in peace, acknowledging conflicts and overcoming them?

As I pondered this, I sat down with my journal. I began to see where I had recorded resolutions to conflicts! I read entries where I had described the unexpected ways God had brought about reconciliation and restoration. The greatest Lover had been at work after all!

Suddenly, quietly, I began to look back on the ways the Prince of Peace has visited me over the past years as I have sought His healing presence and His guidance in those conflicts. Indeed, I have seen others overcome prejudices and presuppositions to join together in mutuality and respect. I have experienced relationships that rose above self-centeredness and control; instead, we learned to cherish and value one another. I have seen children and parents find new ways to get along with each other.

It seems inevitable that where two or three are gathered together, there is often conflict. Yet Jesus said that where two or three are gathered together *in His name,* He would also be there, as an active, powerful, loving presence. This is good news for our relationships.

But how do we do this—this gathering in His name? Let me suggest the practice of *relational prayer.* By this I mean the intentional practicing of the presence of Christ, who exists with us, between us, and among us.

Maybe, just maybe, the Living Christ comes to us now as He did to the two confused pilgrims on the Emmaus Road, to open blind eyes, to soften hard hearts, to defuse power struggles, and to reconcile us, first to Himself and then to each other. Perhaps our conflicts and problems have been exposed because that is where Christ wants to do His work.

Relational prayer is a form of meditation. It turns our attention from our interpersonal problems to the Lord who fixes them. As we deliberately bring the awareness of Christ's presence into our encounters, He changes the way we see them. And that changes the way we act.

Christ's presence empowers us to extend His transforming power to others, in acts and words of love. As we recognize the Prince of Peace in our midst, He works in our relationships. In many practical ways, He guides His children into His image and away from the wider, easier, well-traveled paths of conformity, power playing, and control. Practicing the presence of Christ in our transactions releases His splendor in and through us.

They were right, those scrupulous folks who warned me about meditation. Meditation did indeed get me in trouble. Big trouble. It changed everything.

However, meditation didn't change me in the ways my skeptics feared. It did not "empty my mind," but filled it with the teachings of Christ, as I concentrated on the Scriptures. My daily practice of retreating to an inward sanctuary didn't "move God out of my life." Instead, more and more, I found myself choosing to turn a listening ear to the still, small Voice.

I didn't "drop out" and levitate from place to place in a holy aura. The presence of Christ pushed me out into the lives of other seekers. It united me with other believers. And it led me deeper and deeper into a love for the Bible, with all its richness and life-changing power.

Meditation didn't pull me away from my doctrinal roots. Instead, it gave new meaning and intensity to the doctrines upon which my life was built. I claimed my spiritual heritage not only with Christians through the centuries who have found peace and power in meditation, but also with Isaac, "who meditated in the fields," and David, who "meditated on the laws of God morning and evening," and with Jesus, who frequently drew apart to align Himself with His Heavenly Father.

Practicing the presence of Christ in my daily routine did turn my life upside down, just as they warned me it would. The area where I see the most change is in my relationships. Thank goodness! I came to a new understanding of Henri Nouwen's words: "Conversion to God, therefore, means a simultaneous conversion to the other persons who live and work with you on this earth."

Indeed, it was partly because of my human relationships that

19

I was drawn to the idea and practice of communion with Christ. However, when I began seriously practicing the principles of the contemplative life, I had no way of knowing how profound the effects of Christ's presence would be. I have come to understand that God's renovating presence transforms every human relationship.

It is as if my heart-prayer awakens me to the fault lines upon which I have built my relationships. Visualizing Christ's presence standing between myself and another person somehow exposes the unhealthy dependencies and the self-defeating ways of relating. Desiring to see with Christ's eyes gives me the soft eyes of love instead of the hard eyes of criticism. Longing to think with the mind of Christ, and to love with His love, changes the way I approach every single encounter.

Meditation increases my ability to pay attention to my loved ones. As I attempt to hear their words with an awareness of Christ's love, I can truly hear with my heart. Meditation makes me uncomfortable with manipulation and games—my own and others'. In surrendering my stubborn self-will to God, I come face-to-face with my control issues, and then I am given tools for recovery in those relationships.

Meditation somehow gives me tolerance to allow others' idiosyncrasies and peculiarities. It kneads my brain and heart, permitting me to accept others' uniqueness. Meditation gives me whatever I need to receive the pain of problems, to embrace them as God's teaching aids, to lean into my questions, and to live with uncertainties and contradictions.

As I learned to meditate and later wrote *Creative Silence*, I was beginning my recovery from co-dependence, although I did not know that until the book was finished. Since that process began, it seems as if layer after layer of blindness has been removed from my eyes. I now recognize areas where I need to change in relating to others. <u>The awareness of my own brokenness has become increasingly clear through prayer. I no longer focus on the brokenness of others.</u> This move out of the darkness of denial is the gift of the Reconciler. He exposes the pain that has been there all along, and heals it with His Divine Splendor.

2
Peace . . . and Love

We don't have to understand to know that prayer is love,
and love is never wasted.

—Madeleine L'Engle

A new command I give you: Love one another. As I have
loved you, so you must love one another.

John 13:34

Peace I leave with you, My peace I give to you; not as the
world gives. . . .

John 14:27 NKJV

"Nobody in this family understands how much love I need!"
Amy, our youngest daughter, had had a particularly rough day
and had finally dissolved into wails of anguish. In her frustration,
this five-year-old had spoken truth about the human condition.

At the end of a long and distinguished career, noted historian
Will Durant was interviewed on television. At ninety-two he
said, "My final lesson of history is the same as that of Jesus. You
may think it is a lollipop, but just try it—love one another." The
innocent childhood and seasoned wisdom arrived at the same
conclusion.

Lee Atwater, the notorious "bad boy" of Republican politics,
was interviewed by *Life* magazine (February 1991) shortly before

he died. He had masterminded the nastiest political campaign in history, only to be felled by a brain tumor after George Bush was elected president.

In the gut-wrenching tale of his illness, Atwater spoke of the acquisitive nature of the eighties, and of its accompanying emptiness. The aggressive warrior of political minefields penned out his regrets on the razor's edge between life and death:

> My illness helped me to see what was missing in me: a little heart, a lot of brotherhood. . . . What power wouldn't I trade for a little more time with my family? What price wouldn't I pay for an evening with friends? It took a deadly illness to put me eye to eye with that truth, but it is a truth that the country, caught up in its ruthless ambitions and moral decay, can learn on my dime. I don't know who will lead us through the 90's, but they must be made to speak to this spiritual vacuum at the heart of American society, this tumor of the soul.

Practicing the presence of Christ is not a luxury; it is necessary to our survival. Extending the splendor of Christ's love is no longer a pie-in-the-sky matter; it is vital to our existence.

Each of us has a basic, God-given *need* to love and be loved. Each of us longs to belong to a significant other or others, to have a place where we feel valued and cherished. *And we who call ourselves Christians have been commanded by Christ to love one another.*

So why isn't there more love? And why aren't Christians setting the pace in loving? How can Christians speak the words of Christ and the words of warfare from the same mouths? How can we attend to our collective "tumor of the soul"?

"I made a decision to turn my whole life over to God," the young woman cried over the phone, "and as soon as I did, trouble broke out in every one of my important relationships.

Shouldn't Christians have things worked out better than this?"

"I try so hard to get close to others," another friend told me, "but it seems that the harder I try, the more people avoid me."

In preparing for his role in the movie *Rain Man*, Dustin Hoffman conducted serious research in the area of autism. In an interview, the noted actor commented that he thinks our nation is in danger of becoming "spiritually autistic." In other words, we are becoming so self-absorbed that we are in danger of becoming incapable of relating to each other. This is true among Christians, as well. Conformed to the culture, we feed the same tumors of materialism and hatred.

A lovely young woman flounced out of a counseling session, leaving her husband to pick up the pieces of his life. "I don't need this!" was her final word to her husband and the minister. What she meant was that she was not willing to go through the inevitable struggles of learning how to give and take. She did not care to grapple with the complexities of living intimately. The marriage that was inherently "good" died because of an unwillingness to pay the price of wholeness. Indeed, one of the common causes of marital failure seems to be an unwillingness to learn how to love with what C. S. Lewis calls "gift-love," instead of "need-love." We cling to those who offer the love we need, just as long as we need it. But we will not give love if it is difficult or unprofitable to do so.

I hear cries of loneliness and alienation day after day from everyday, normal folks. Some want to get along better with others. Some just want a place to belong. Accompanying the sense of isolation is a corresponding shame that says, "I *should* be able to be close," or, "There must be something wrong with me."

Any bookstore in town is filled with how-to books for getting all the love you need. Yet many are trying to figure out how to get out of relationships they are in or into relationships they think they want. Those who have chosen to stay involved with others

The presence of Christ will affect every area of life. Painful – but good

Peace . . . and Love

Wounds of love.

often experience turmoil and conflict instead of joy and fulfillment.

"I've wounded so many others and I have been wounded. Is there a way to start over without moving across the continent?" A lovely young woman's heartfelt expression moved me to consider the harm we do to each other in these days of instant intimacy and counterfeit closeness. Can Christ's redemptive power heal these wounds?

Within the last twenty years, there has been a flood of research done on relationships. Within the burgeoning recovery field, researchers have learned that, when one spouse begins recovering from an addiction—to food, work, alcohol, drugs, fear, rage, or whatever has control of the person—the entire family unit is set spinning. Family therapists discovered that, when the recovering partner begins to change, the entire family system undergoes great stress. Often the "sober" spouse is not able to stand the recovery and the marriage dissolves. Thus a new term was born— the field of "co-dependency" exploded, giving insight and help for the entire family.

My own experience validates the findings of family therapists. Entering into a deep prayer life was the catalyst for a spiritual recovery for me. When I got serious about becoming responsible for my own life and when I entered into a serious effort of contemplative prayer, the very foundations of my relationships were challenged. Practicing the presence of Christ led to what Carl Jung called "individuation"—becoming my own person, responsible and mature. That process has touched every facet of my life.

In an almost predictable pattern, my friendships, my marriage, my family life, my church life, and my work relationships began to change. I began to see my own faults and character defects. The areas where I was immature and selfish and self-serving became crystal clear.

Suddenly, with painful realizations, I began to identify the self-defeating patterns, the indirect and nonproductive communication styles, and I was practically shoved out of the darkness of denial into the light of the Truth of Christ. Over and over, I have been caught by surprise, just as those disciples were on the Emmaus Road. Instead of entering a state of euphoria or nirvana, I followed Christ's Spirit on a difficult road where I hadn't dreamed of going.

I had always wanted to see myself as a loving and giving person. I had a high investment in maintaining my image of myself as selfless and kind. Suddenly, I saw that I had a highly polished shell of self-confidence that I showed to the world, but my true self was different. That shell was hiding a frightened little child who had managed to close her emotional doors in order to please others.

Practicing the presence of Christ began a process of opening the doors to the fresh wind of the Spirit of Love. Once I began opening those doors to honesty and transparency, I discovered that I was not alone. Many others like me—fellow Christians who were struggling to make connections with others—had also closed their emotional doors.

I have been particularly good at hiding behind my "pink-dress image." Several years ago, I was making my first venture out in teaching Sunday school with a new friend. One warm spring morning, much to my horror, a problem erupted in our department.

Since I was highly skilled in avoiding conflict and looking good, I was mortified at the prospect of being caught at the scene of a conflict at church, of all places. My discomfort mounted that afternoon when the minister in charge of that particular area asked my friend and me to visit him on Monday morning to discuss this situation.

It didn't matter that I was not directly involved in this uproar, but was merely a witness. It never occurred to me that this *au-*

thority figure, meek and mild though he was, held no malice in his heart and that there was nothing he could do to me. I told myself all Sunday afternoon and evening that all he wanted were facts, but I still terrorized myself with worry about what he might think of me for being witness to a conflict.

On Monday morning, then, with no special awareness of what I was doing with my clothing, I put on my pink dress with lace and delicate embroidery trim and drove over to pick up my part-ner in crime, the other teacher. She, too, came dressed for the battle in—you guessed it—a frilly pink dress! We laughed self-consciously at our ploy and the nonverbal message we wanted to send. And we got ourselves a name for the game we had both learned to play so well: *people-pleasing*.

People-pleasing was one of the first ways I began building a wall between myself and others. The habit started at a very early age. I suppose I began building walls and closing emotional doors when someone laughed at me and I felt silly or dumb.

Even at this moment, I can recall the excruciating pain of shyness when I was very young. I must have feared that I wouldn't or couldn't "perform" right or well enough or perfectly. I remem-ber hiding behind my mother's skirts in paralyzing terror when I was going into a new place. The fear of not measuring up en-gulfed me early.

Even though I often felt different or out of step, I didn't want anyone to know how different I really was, and so I developed ways to cover up those feelings. Even now, it is a source of unending relief to me when I watch a fellow pilgrim discover that she, too, always felt "different."

Sometimes I still feel that archaic, childhood shyness. It crops up when I am going into a place with unfamiliar people, even though I have learned many techniques for hiding those fears. When this occurs, however, I feel as though I am five years old all over again, and I find myself hiding behind other masks, wishing I had my mother's skirts and her protection again.

I find it exciting and freeing to learn how those walls have been built. Only through Christ's mercy can we even recognize the problem. And once we discover the dynamics that make us hide within those prisons of fear and anger, that discovery can be the door that leads to forgiveness and change. I am seeing how powerful the forces of fear are in creating insurmountable barriers between people who desperately want to love each other. Often these are Christians, who wonder how in the world they can be so alienated when they have supposedly been redeemed by the Living Christ.

Walls both result from and lead to control problems and power struggles in relationships. Walls, born out of distrust, create even more fear and distrust. Walls make cold churches and dysfunctional families. Walls create children who don't understand what it is to love and be loved. A walled-in person might as well wear a sign that says, "I'm scared to come out."

Part of the joy of learning how to love has been in learning that even my closest friends have often hidden their true selves behind closed doors. Together, we are discovering through spiritual growth groups how to take the risk of being transparent. We are finding that, while little children often shut their emotional doors, the power of Christ's transforming and healing love can open those doors once again.

We gather each week in a circle of chairs. One by one, we who may appear to be strong and efficient and "together" muster the courage to reveal our broken, wounded, scarred, and scared selves to one another. In the caring for one another, the curing happens.

While these spiritual growth groups are not therapy groups, again and again we discover the therapeutic gift of Christ's presence among us. While the groups are not prayer groups, we are

28

keenly aware that our conversation itself is prayer and that Christ is speaking to us through each other. We take seriously the responsibility of praying for one another during the week as well. And even though these groups are not for the purpose of Bible study, we base our work on biblical principles, particularly the principles of Christ and His teachings.

In our caring for each other, the walls do come tumbling down. We learn how to live within *boundaries* instead of walls. We allow the Spirit of Christ to build bridges between us so that we may be united. We are learning what it is to make peace instead of war. <u>We are also discovering the difference between keeping the peace, which is a way of staying in the hiding place of denial and dishonesty, and *making* peace, which is about showing love</u>. As each of us draws closer to the love of Christ, we experience over and over those Emmaus Road moments when truth breaks through the darkness and shows us something about freedom in love.

"I see! I see!" one of the group members almost yelled at the rest of us one bright spring day. We have been meeting together for years now, and there is a great deal of safety among us. "I see that I have been playing the victim with this person, and *I don't have to do that anymore!*" Blind eyes were opened as she continued to walk in the presence of Christ.

"I didn't know I was so dishonest," cried another group member after she saw the places where she had abused and mistreated her friends. "I didn't realize I was hurting others, because I have been so focused on what others have done to me." Sometimes those Emmaus Road moments hurt as the truth breaks open a part of a frightened heart.

If Jesus Christ has called us to anything, I believe He has called us to <u>a life of love</u>. The longer I live, the more I see that *the* call of Christ is to love one another, and yet it is so much easier to try to control others or to be controlled by each other. The call is to love, and yet it must seem so hard to love that most of us merely try to get power over each other. If the call is to love, why is it that so many of us cower in hideouts of fear?

I could, if I chose, scare myself out of friendships just by listening to my neighbors talk about how hard it is to get along. If I decided to, I could frighten myself into pulling down the shades, locking all my doors, and staying in my own safe cocoon, just by reading the newspaper and scanning the statistics about divorce, AIDS, lawsuits among former friends, and hostile take-overs.

If I wanted to justify my fears, I could use the failed relationships in my past as proof positive that getting along is risky business. I wouldn't have to use any "fatal attractions" to convince myself that people are a problem. I could use dysfunctional families and tainted business relationships, conflict-ridden churches and fragmented political parties, as clear documentation. And then I could cite magazine and newspaper articles that explore the growing problem of loneliness in our society. After all that, I could shrug my shoulders and claim that I am just a product of my society.

The truth is that many of us human beings in this enlightened age are afraid to love, often because we know that love will change us. We know that we will be disappointed in love, and some are honest enough to admit that we will disappoint the very ones we love most. We will be betrayed and we will betray. We will get tired of others, and they will tire of us. We will want to give up on others, and they will want to give up on us.

We *will* be disillusioned in love, and that is good! Disillusionment means that the blinders will fall. The false images will crumble. The ego will be stripped away so that the real person God created can emerge. The coming of disillusionment can be the prelude to celebration, for that is when one can begin the process of re-visioning and growing a real love, an incarnational love. Disillusionment can be the experience of the Emmaus Road . . . and the beginning of the walk into true peace and love.

Indeed, I *could* scare myself into isolation and loneliness. I hear clearly the self-serving and self-protective messages of a broken, bleeding world. But out of the madness of my day, I hear another, clearer call. I hear a call to reconciliation. Out of the clamor of the rational, cynical, self-absorbed world, another Voice calls for healing and restoring, and that Voice says, "Follow me. . . ."

I am fascinated by the final words of Jesus to His disciples, as John recorded them. During those last hours, Jesus didn't instruct those faithful friends in doctrine. He didn't give them a procedure for setting up an organization, getting ahead, or "positioning" themselves to win (even though they tried to the very end to get Him to play by those rules). Nor did Jesus lecture them on what they should or shouldn't do or think or feel or be.

In those tender moments before the crucifixion, Jesus spoke to the disciples as one would talk to family members or beloved friends when the end is near. Jesus spoke to His loved ones in *relational* terms. He said such things as, "Abide in me," and, "Love one another." He gently admonished them to serve each other and to stay connected to each other.

I believe that the call of Christ then and now is a call to transforming relationships. I believe that Christ wants Christians to be different in the ways we get along with each other. I believe that the One who set it all up in the first place calls for greater integrity and honesty, better communication, deeper commitment, and more joy and delight.

And I believe that acceptance of the Christ-life means that the magnificence and splendor of Christ's love comes to each of us, transforming us, making us instruments of His peace and love and joy. I believe He has called us to share the splendor of His

31

presence in a world that is starving to death for meaningful belonging.

When that image of Christ is consciously and consistently held
up among the partners in any relationship, a power is set loose
that heals and binds. A re-visioning of the relationship breaks the
vise grip of control issues and self-seeking, leading instead to true
intimacy. Prayer, that quiet prayer of the heart where Christ is
held in focus in the mind and heart of the pray-er, can indeed
change things, even relationships.

Is merely *praying* a viable solution for brokenness among people?

It's such a simple thing to do—so simple that some who want
a more sophisticated method might overlook it.

Can something so simple really work? Will it really change
things to simply hold, in my mind's eye, a picture of myself and
another in the presence of Christ?

What good would it possibly do to see myself handing over my
husband or my child or my friend into the hands of the Creator?

Do I dare pray for my loved ones or for those with whom I am
in conflict with nothing in mind but for the redemptive work of
Christ to be released between us and among us? Do I have the
courage to pray with no agenda and allow Christ to pray His
agenda to me and through us? Do I dare trust the presence of the
Living Christ to heal what is broken in my associations with other
human beings? Can friendship with Christ really bring about
reconciliation?

Contemplative relationships? Christ-with-us now as in history?
Fact or fantasy?

I won't know until I try.

What have I got to lose? What have I got to gain?

3
The Third Party

Christianity is the acceptance of the gift of the friendship of Jesus.

—Leslie Weatherhead

If anyone loves me, he will obey my teaching. My Father will love him, and we will come to him and make our home with him.

John 14:23

———⬥———

"I've tried everything."

The voice on the other end of the phone was quiet, but desperate. "I have psychological understanding," she continued, "but it has given me understanding and not real change. I have read countless books and gone to seminars. Do you think God could help me get along better with others?"

Another voice recounted an amazing process of recovery. "I have discovered that the Higher Power has a name, and His name is God. Until I tapped into the power of the Living Christ, I really didn't understand anything!"

A proponent of the New Age movement discovered that her "highest self" wasn't high enough to solve the common, everyday problems that beset the best of families. "If I'm the highest power I've got to call on, I'm in big trouble!"

Several years ago, I had a problem with a particularly troublesome friendship between two people in one of my spiritual growth groups. I analyzed it with all my best knowledge and called on the counsel of a trusted authority. I took responsibility for my part of the problem. More than once, I took the initiative to make things better, admitting that I was powerless over the other persons.

Frankly, even with all my best efforts, that problem wouldn't budge. I was stuck in blocked communication and there didn't seem to be any hope for resolving the problem. Hopelessness and helplessness were growing every day, and I was close to giving up.

My usual response when something I am doing in a relationship is not working is to turn up the volume on the very thing that isn't working! If a little bit doesn't work, I will do a whole lot. This is similar to pushing my hand down to the bottom of a pot of boiling water when I sense the water is hot!

If yelling at my children doesn't make them pick up their rooms, I will yell louder. If continuing to badger my husband, Martus, about a fault doesn't make him change, I will badger more. When withdrawing in a cold huff doesn't make a friend come running to me with pleas for forgiveness, I withdraw even further into my shell. If working hard to please someone who doesn't like me doesn't soften up the person, I just work harder and harder to change his opinion of me. I'll make that sourpuss like me if it kills me!

All the time I'm working hard at trying to control another's opinion of me, I'm getting more and more dishonest and duplicitous. All of the energy I expend to people-please (or to get power over one who is working equally hard to escape my power) wears me out and makes me angrier and angrier. That's when I want to give up and walk out of the relationship.

When I am tempted to give up on a relationship, it feels like a personal failure. I do a good bit of self-bashing, forgetting to take into account that the other person shares part of the responsibility for the problem. Even if I have done everything I know to do and it is clear that the other person doesn't want to meet me halfway or any other way, I still tend to think that things would have worked out if I could have done more or been more or been better, smarter, or nicer.

Through the practice of relational praying, I am learning that the better way is to <u>continue to bring myself and that person to Christ in prayer. Without praying for a specific thing to happen, but laying down my expectations of what should happen in this relationship, I continue to imagine the three of us—my problem person, Christ, and myself—standing together in the warmth of love and acceptance</u>.

Over and over, I visualize this scene of the three of us. I try to envision what Christ must be saying to each of us as He attempts to open our eyes to His presence and power. In the situation described earlier, there was no movement or change in my imaginary picture for many weeks. Even though there was no perceptible change in either of us, I continued to picture those of us involved in the problem as if we were together. Frankly, I had exhausted all other possibilities, so I had no recourse but to surrender in prayer.

Life doesn't automatically fall into place in peace and harmony just because I want it to. Part of the reason for this, I think, is that God must continually show me that *He* is God! Furthermore, He must work within the context of my own resistance, my own character defects, and those of others, and sometimes I make God's job of reconciliation most difficult.

I'm not about to change my mind until you do! I found myself thinking privately when locked in a battle of wills with another person. I couldn't believe that such immaturity was coming from me, and yet there I was, holding on with a death grip to my way of dealing with a problem. My self-will was operating at full tilt!

Sometimes when I am practicing the presence of Christ in a relationship, I have to admit that I am not ready to give up my

35

part of the battle. I have to ask to be made willing. There are times when I have to ask for the grace to *want* to forgive the other person or to accept forgiveness for myself.

Often, I cannot see what the problem is, and so I must pray for clarity. At times, I must admit that reconciliation is so improbable by human efforts that only the direct intervention of Christ's power can bring about healing. I believe that even the ability to be honest about my own unwillingness is evidence of Christ's presence and activity.

It is hard for me to take my hands off a situation and not work to fix and control it. My arrogance and pride sometimes seduce me into thinking that I know what is best for all parties concerned. Not doing anything but merely *praying* seems too inconsequential for one who believes in doing something, even if it's wrong!

"I don't like that, Michelle," I stormed at my oldest daughter in a firm tone on a hot summer day following her graduation. I felt a strong need to change her behavior. Fuming, I drew myself up into my commander-in-chief persona and prepared to launch my attack.

"I know you don't, Mother," she said serenely, almost sweetly, and then she simply walked away, leaving me with eyes opened by her calm response. Michelle taught me that I must lay down my control of her and let her grow into her adulthood. I had been praying about our relationship, but the answer didn't come as I had expected.

I am learning, though slowly, and the way I am learning is in coming up square against the things I cannot change and the people I cannot control. The painful thorns of some relationships allow Christ to do His work and reveal His power. In mysterious ways, God opens the doors between us. His Spirit is indeed an active, penetrating agent.

The Christ who comes to us comes with His own healing

agenda, and He fits the healing process to the need—just as He did when He walked the earth. Jesus Christ comes with the intention of bringing about wholeness among us, and He has many ways of bringing us into the light of His love.

Christ Comes as Teacher

> I will ask the Father, and he will give you another Counselor to be with you forever—the Spirit of truth. . . .
>
> John 14:16, 17

The Living Christ comes to give instructions and nudge us toward truth. He uses people and events and problems to teach us. The spiritual disciplines of daily prayer, meditation, and Bible study, added to our communion with other seekers, all provide the necessary framework for those moments of inspiration.

God's teaching is clearest to me when I stay in consistent and regular communication with Him, taking in messages through the spiritual disciplines. Now and then, He bursts through with special moments of grace to make some lesson clear.

For years, Martus and I have taught a course in Couples' Communication to married couples. We have our tools and techniques down pat, but we continue to refine and refresh our teaching. We tone up our theories and polish our presentations to make sure the couples learn the principles of talking together. Sometimes we are the learners!

Martus and I enjoy teaching communication principles, whether it is in a mini-session after a Marriage Enrichment banquet, or in a six-week intensive seminar with practice and homework. We enjoy the process of preparing and presenting because we believe that good communication is a vital responsibility for Christians. Through the years of carving out our own relationships, we have seen the value of straightforward communication. For us, communication is not work, but fun.

One night in Abilene, Texas, we were on a roll. For some reason, everything was clicking. Our examples were spontaneous and on target, and the audience responded warmly and enthusiastically. In modeling conflict resolution about time priorities, Martus and I were defining an issue for the group, and suddenly what had for years been a problem in dealing with time suddenly became clear to both of us—right up there in front of everyone! Both of us saw our tug-of-war of wills, and suddenly, in a flash of inspiration, we had the will to make a change.

Over and over (often while we are up before a group modeling a technique), we have become aware of a Power greater than ourselves. Suddenly, almost imperceptibly, we are aware that the Christ has met each of us at the point of our own need and, perhaps, brokenness. As we have worked through the sometimes awkward process of identifying what the real issue of conflict is, we have been shown a way of moving toward each other. In a breakdown of communication, we have suddenly moved through an impasse to new understanding and closeness.

Typical definitions of *prayer* would not include those moments. Certainly, there is nothing that either of us is doing overtly that would suggest a formal prayer. Nevertheless, we become aware of the presence of Christ when we move toward a place of peace. It is indeed a holy moment when Christ's invading love reveals truth. It is indeed a holy space when Christ's intervening presence takes over.

How can I be sure that Christ is speaking to us in those moments? Because I have made a decision to surrender my will and my life *and my relationships* to Christ, and because I know that my husband has as well. Therefore, we trust God to break into our experiences when He chooses to do so. We accept these times as special gifts of grace.

The Teacher often enrolls me in His night school, either waking me up from a deep sleep or keeping me awake. I usually resist that class! After all, I am a very busy person and need my sleep to fulfill all my important responsibilities! However, since I am often so busy and focused on my own agenda during the day, the Instructor has to catch me off guard, waking me up to work through a troubling issue, guiding me to a book or a Scripture I need to read, or simply calling me to prayer. Sometimes, too, I am awakened suddenly with an answer to a problem or a heading for a chapter. The Teacher does what He has to do when He has to do it.

Christ Comes as Servant

> He poured water into a basin and began to wash his disciples' feet, drying them with the towel that was wrapped around him.
>
> John 13:5

I have friends who have walked through the thick underbrush of my life with me for several years. They have been there to encourage me when I have been afraid to venture out. They have listened when I have been sorting through circumstances, attempting to find the way of Christ. And they have given me physical relief at times when I was weary or ill. Sometimes their acts of mercy have felt to me like a kind of foot-washing.

The Servant Christ comes to me in human flesh again and again to give me exactly what I need. Last week over lunch, Mary Ellen told me of an experience she had in growing up, and suddenly I had a much-needed tool for relating to one of my children. Annette lent me a book that gave me insight and direction for conducting my business. Charlotte spent hours of each week during the past year helping me with the nuts and bolts of my office, so that I could carry on with my work, and Ann brought dinner for my family on a particularly busy day.

The Servant Christ knows exactly how each of us needs to be served. This serving comes at exactly the right time, and through His willing instruments. The growing edge for me is not only to be aware of the times and ways He is coming to me through His human instruments, but also to be sensitive to the ways He wants to use me in service to others. Prayer wakes me up to the needs of others and then gives me specific guidance in meeting those needs.

The Servant Christ comes to help in private ways that have a public effect. Last winter, I was trying to regain my strength after a bout with the flu. I was working on a lecture I was to deliver at our Community Bible Study, and I could not come up with an introduction that fit.

Finally, worn-out and frustrated, I decided to take a brief rest. As I lay down, I poured out my frustration in prayer. I left nothing unsaid about my weariness, and I ended with a petulant statement about how I didn't believe God cared much about me or He would come to my aid.

I slept hard for ten minutes, waking refreshed—and with the perfect introduction. Perhaps it was in my imagination, but it seemed as if I could hear God chuckling and saying, "I'm glad you finally told me the truth. Now, here's your introduction for Wednesday's lecture."

Christ Comes as Physician

> It is not the healthy who need a doctor, but the sick. I have not come to call the righteous, but sinners to repentance.
>
> Luke 5:31, 32

Sandra Hulse, my soul friend along the spiritual journey to wholeness, always seems to know the exact words I need to hear when I am hurting. She has never once given me pity or sympathy, nor has she shamed me for hurting, telling me I "shouldn't" feel the way I do. Instead, she applies a healing principle or truth to the area of my pain. I leave our encounters knowing the tenderness of the Great Physician, who works through human instruments.

As I listen to others and to my own heart, I am becoming aware of a new need. We need to be healed of harmful memories from the past, so that we can be freed to truly love people in the present. In prayer, those old, binding memories can be healed. Just as the Good Samaritan bound the wounds of the man left by the roadside to die, so the Living Christ comes to heal the broken places in my own heart so that I can love more freely.

"I can't get the memory of my parents' fighting out of my mind," confided Sarah, a brilliant young woman. "When I was little, I would lie in my bed and tremble and cry, wishing they would not fight and hoping they would not hurt each other."

Over and over, Sarah relived that memory with the other group members. She talked about it repeatedly, until she got tired of hearing herself wallow in the past. Finally, she was ready to visualize Christ's walking into her bedroom, taking her in His arms, and comforting her. Eventually, the presence of Christ in that memory became more powerful than the voice of angry parents.

Christ Comes as Friend

> I no longer call you servants, because a servant does not know his master's business. Instead, I have called you friends, for everything that I learned from my Father I have made known to you.
>
> John 15:15

"How can I show Linda the constancy of Christ's love?" I asked my husband about a lovely young woman whose fear of abandonment was causing her to abandon others before they had a chance to leave her. She had asked for spiritual direction, though she wasn't really sure she "believed."

"Just show up, week after week," Martus counseled me, "and show her that you aren't going to leave her."

I began to recall my own faithful friends who had never left me, even though I feel sure they might have wanted to. I recalled one special friend who had met with me week after week as I worked through a program of recovery. I remembered how she was always available when I needed her and how she never acted too busy when I called. Her faithfulness has taught me much about the friendship of Christ, for in her presence I came to experience the warmth and constancy of Christ's presence.

Another woman, Brenda, attended a spiritual growth group, but had to sit by the door in each meeting. She was so intensely uncomfortable with even the physical closeness of the room that she wanted to guarantee a speedy exit.

Week after week she came and sat near her escape exit. I knew we had made great progress in creating safety for Brenda when she chose to sit opposite the door. Now I see Brenda intermingling freely with others, smiling, and helping others to feel at home in a strange place. The Friend-God worked through human friends to transform this lonely, fearful person into a gentle and communicative friend to others. *That is shared splendor!*

There have been many times when I have become acutely aware of the Friend Jesus who stands between my loved ones and me, revealing joy and delight in the process of living together. His friendship enhances every other friendship I have. Seeing Christ between myself and another person somehow lifts that relationship to a new level of intimacy and sharing. I don't know for sure how that works. I only know that it does.

I have watched Martus express the nature of Christ in his pastoral life. He often stands as friend in the crises of our church members, quietly giving support and comfort, making necessary phone calls, taking care of details, and listening to the words of troubled or grief-stricken family members. I have also watched him rejoice in the birth of a new life, the joyful celebrations of families, and in the business and personal accomplishments of those whom he has befriended in the name of Christ.

Christ Comes as Transformer

> I am the resurrection and the life. He who believes in me will live, even though he dies; and whoever lives and believes in me will never die. . . .
>
> John 11:25, 26

"Little people talk about other people," my father would tell me over and over, "but big people talk about ideas." My father was filled with pithy sayings and good advice. He always encouraged me to rise above gossip and idle chatter, and to think on "whatsoever things are lovely." Daddy had no tolerance for slander or slight, and he never did like to hear about the latest scandal. He held his mind on higher, nobler things, no matter how cleverly the rest of us tried to draw him into our people-bashing.

My mother, too, urged me to follow the scriptural teaching that "as a man thinketh in his heart, so is he." Through long years of living on the growing edges of a vibrant faith, my mother learned that change comes as that inner kingdom is yielded to the Father's hand. Only in living "in Christ," that is, being a "practicing Christian," does true transformation come.

I have noticed that when I gather with others "in His name"— with the awareness that He is present—there is a different atmosphere. The conversation is lifted to a level beyond pettiness and emptiness.

I am amazed, too, at how quickly rapport is established when both parties are willing to claim a vital relationship with Christ. Just last week, I met a stranger for lunch, but within moments, she had established that she was attempting to live with the awareness of Christ and under His direction. She didn't talk holy talk; in fact, her language was the language of a recovering alcoholic whose very sobriety depends on a daily surrender to the agenda of the Higher Power we know as God. We connected immediately at a deep spiritual level because we both had come with the awareness that we were there by divine appointment.

The Third Party Comes as First Priority

> Seek first his kingdom and his righteousness, and all these things will be given to you as well.
>
> Matthew 6:33

This Third Party can and will transform the most problematic of all relationships, but there is a condition to the transformation: He must come first.

When I am not paying attention to the presence of Christ, I decide how the relationship must be, and then I call Him in as a consultant. I tell Him what I want Him to do (which usually means how I want Him to change the other person), and then I sit back and wait for Him to act on my behalf.

In my arrogance and pride, I pick and meddle with the other person. I gaze at the problem, scrutinizing with a critical eye each and every part of the faults and failings of the other party. Now and then, when I remember to do so, I glance at Christ, tossing a demanding prayer in the direction of the Reconciler. I can say without hesitation that reconciliation almost never takes place with that plan.

Finally, I must remember that I am called to seek Christ's rule in my life *first*. I am to put Him first in my affections, and not the other person. I am not to make an idol of the relationship or the problem, worshiping it, feeding it, focusing on it until I have no room in my vision for the work of the One who wants to set things straight.

Repeatedly, the Disturber comes to show me the places where I have deified the relationship (or my will in that relationship). He comes to show me that I must give my first attention, my best affection, and my prior loyalty to Him, and *then* He will work His work of grace and peace. And He usually has a much better plan than any I could have designed.

That Third Party *will* be in charge. He is the one who wants to form each relationship, because He knows best how it should work. He knows what He intends to create in the relationship and how He wants to transform each party within that relationship. He wants to correct the transactions that hurt either party.

The Living Christ longs to give new, peace-making tools for freer communication and spontaneity. He wants to heal whatever wound is hurting the relationship. He wants to make that wound a place of healing for others who are hurting in the same way. And He wants to participate in the freeing of love among friends. It is the Father's *good pleasure*, Jesus told us, to give us the keys to the Kingdom.

The Third Party comes, sometimes boldly and sometimes gently, to open blind eyes and soften hardened hearts. What does the Teacher want to teach you? How does He want to transform your viewpoint and change the way you talk to yourself about others?

Where is the Servant Christ attempting to serve you? What does He want to give you? Does He want to fill you with His love, washing your feet through another person so that you can love others better?

What wounds is the Great Physician trying to heal in you?

Do you think that the Living Christ just might be trying to be your friend?

4
The Face in the Mirror

We all know also that unless we attend to our inner conflicts and contradictions, not only will we find ourselves torn apart by our inner divisions, but also we shall very likely inflict wounds on those around us.

—Esther de Waal

For you created my inmost being; you knit me together in my mother's womb.

Psalm 139:13

Loud, raucous rock music exploded in the auditorium of Angelo State University. The touring company of *Godspell* shook the rafters of the building. The sounds rose and built with intensity. The atmosphere came alive with electric anticipation.

Strobe lights pierced the darkness. Brilliant reds, yellows, and oranges flashed before my shocked eyes. The pastel hues of the pictures in my childhood Bible stood in pale contrast to these throbbing hues. John the Baptist, or at least his contemporary impersonator, burst onto the stage, scattering the old pictures in my head.

"Prepare ye the way of the Lord!" Rapid movement and choral energy filled the stage, assaulting my senses through the first few minutes of this modern musical. The vivid sensory impressions embedded themselves forever in my memory, along with the words of the message: "Repent! Turn around!"

Never again would I have a flat, colorless impression of John the Baptist. I was thunderstruck by the virility and vitality of the preparer of the way. That moment in my history remains a visual reminder of the way God sometimes stuns me to get my attention.

I wasn't any more prepared for the internal renovation God would do through my journey in prayer than I had been for the Baptist's startling appearance on stage. I hadn't counted on the conflicts in relationships that He would bring to my attention. Some of them burst into my life, boiling up suddenly and without warning. Other conflicts were the same-old-same-old, those irritating defects I deal with day after day.

The more I moved into the life of contemplative prayer, the more uncomfortable I became with the status quo of my relationships. In addition, the more I attempted to be aware of Christ's presence in my encounters, the more conflicts there seemed to be. I was disillusioned in some relationships, disappointed and defeated in others. The more I prayed, the more my eyes were opened to the conflicts.

I began to notice, too, that I seemed to have the same conflicts about the same things over and over. Even when I prayed about those conflicts, they persisted. The more I tried to force them out, the more stubbornly they clung. The more I tried to change myself and my transactions, the more difficulty I created for myself.

A "John the Baptist" person pointed out that I habitually had conflicts with the same personality types. I seemed drawn to strong authority figures, and I regularly seemed to get my feelings hurt by those folks. I was also drawn to people who appealed to my "helper" image, only to discover that I needed to help more than the other person wanted to be helped. The names would change, but the situations remained the same.

"If something is going on between two people," I heard a speaker say, "it is because *both parties have agreed to the situation.*" I became concerned about my part in various games and rackets—guilt and shame now joined my fear and anger. How, I wondered, was I going to be an instrument of God's grace if I couldn't even get the conflicts out of my own life?

I was shooting myself in the foot! The splendor of Christ that I longed to share was distorted and thwarted not by others' actions, but by my own. This awareness began to bubble up into my consciousness. The Spirit of Truth was working on the outside to show me what He wanted to do on the inside, and that was a remodeling job.

Slowly, I also began to catch on to the fact that I was neither the villain nor the innocent. I began to see that nobody else could make me feel, think, or do anything. If I continued with my relational praying, Christ's Spirit was going to force me to admit my own responsibility in things.

Implicit within every problem, whether a minor skirmish or a true crisis, is an invitation for me to repent and turn around. Within every conflict, there is a question that God is asking me. Within every burden is an opportunity for a blessing. If I remain in intimate friendship with God, He shows me the sometimes painful truth about my problems.

When I began this inner journey, I didn't know that God would transform me, and I was frightened at the forces that shook the foundations of my life. I had much to learn about the ego, that outward persona or mask that seemed "real." I was to learn, though, that "dying to self" involved a radical change, and that my ego was part of what had to die. Nor did I know that, as in any other death, I would go through predictable stages. I regularly repeated the typical grief process that occurs with any transition.

Giving up the old wineskins was a death, and it hurt and scared me because I had no way of knowing what new thing was being born.

Looking back, I see the pattern I repeat when a "John the Baptist" experience bursts into my life. First, I **deny** the problem, often giving up my prayer life for a season because it is too uncomfortable to be confronted in the silence. However, I eventually return to prayer—either because my discomfort grows too great, or because I feel a gnawing guilt about the commitment I have made.

Oswald Chambers teaches that God continually brings up the same problem in our lives until we finally decide to deal with it. A well-marked passage in my frayed copy of Chambers's classic, *My Utmost for His Highest*, says,

> In numberless ways God will bring us back to the same point over and over again. He never tires of bringing us to the one point until we learn the lesson, because he is producing the finished product.

At some point, when I can't stick my head in sand deep enough, I enter the **anger** stage of grief, I lash out at others, always finding someone else to blame for my pain. I attack and play games of "If only . . ." and "What if . . . ?" I long for someone to rescue me, only to discover, in prayer, that God's intent is far more than rescue—He wants to deliver me from bondage.

The next stage of transition is the **bargaining** stage. This is when the researcher in me goes into full action. At this stage, I think I can outsmart the problem and outfox God. I read books and collect articles, go to seminars and talk to others about how they solve similar problems.

This bargaining stage isn't all bad, for it provides me with tools and insights that help me cooperate with God in making changes.

Sometimes, too, this stage can be good in forcing necessary changes, getting me to do some things I may have needed to do all along. However, bargaining, too, can become a form of denial and hiding from the truth.

Some folks' bargaining tactics revolve around changing spouses or jobs or geographical locations. They may spend more money, consult another counselor, try *one more* diet or medical treatment, or join a different church—anything to fix the situation!

Finally, in my case, when I see that I can't read enough or learn enough or move fast enough to outrun the problem, I move into the stage of **depression,** turning in on myself in a desperate kind of self-blaming and anger. A part of me is beginning to realize that true change is coming, and the old part, enslaved to my ego, holds on in a death grip, hoping to avoid the inevitable change.

In some areas of my life, I can traverse the slippery slopes of change in a short time. In others, I take years. The length of time seems to hinge on how quickly I return to my discipline of prayer. The power of the Living Christ in my life is connected to the consistency of my listening to God's promptings.

In my life of relational prayer, I have learned that God allows "John the Baptist" experiences to burst into my life to shake me up. Within those times of suffering, He invites me to give up my attachments to things, people, and ideas that keep me from that deeper, primary attachment to Him. Within every crisis, God is beckoning me to lay down my ego, to take myself off the throne of my own life, and to trust Him.

There are times when, in the midst of brokenness and pain with those I love most, I have heard that still, small Voice reassuring me. In love, and in His own time, the Living Christ finally brings me to the point of **acceptance.** That is the moment when I finally admit the problem and call it by its name. Acceptance is that moment of blessed relief when I quit running from the truth. It is when I am willing to own my responsibility in it. I am finally willing to be changed. Acceptance is that act of humility in which I admit that only God is all-powerful.

In prayer, the paths between myself and others are made straight. In the process of repenting, I discover that the hills, those seemingly insurmountable problems, are made flat and that the valleys, those deep and dark pits of isolation, are lifted into the light of peace. I also become better acquainted with my ego.

I sat at my dressing table one cold winter day, looking into the mirror as if at a stranger. Who was this person looking back at me? And was it the person others saw? Could others see beyond my mask to the real me, and if they could, what did they think?

Or, more accurately, which one of my selves was the real me anyway? Scanning my face, I realized that I was a stranger to myself and that the real self that God created was hiding behind an outer shell that was beginning to crumble. In the process of prayer, Christ's spirit would open my eyes to the many protective layers of my ego and the fear that kept it all in place. *Then* I would begin to love more freely.

Very early, children decide whether the universe is a friendly place or a hostile one. At a young age, a child decides whether he is going to trust himself and distrust the world, or trust the world and distrust himself. From that decision, the ego begins to form, shaping his decisions and his destiny.

At a certain level, ego is necessary and vital to survival. Ego development is part of our natural maturation process. This helps me understand who I am, distinct from others.

But if a child decides to distrust himself, to hide from the world, the ego can become a false defense mechanism. In this case, the ego is not a healthy self-awareness, but a mask. It is an image presented to the world.

We can easily find ourselves hiding behind these images, well into adulthood. As long as we play certain games with those around us, we don't have to be honest about who we really are. In this way, our egos can dupe us into misconceptions about ourselves and others—sometimes even about God.

I didn't know all of this when I began my spiritual growth process. If you had asked me what kind of person I wanted to be, I'd have said that I wanted to be noticed and admired. Of course, I had my faults, but I hoped people would overlook them.

But as my spiritual growth progressed, I learned some bothersome things about myself. I discovered that the "me" others saw wasn't always what I wanted them to see. I would try to present a carefully polished image, but I was realizing that this image was false. Either I was lying about myself or I just didn't know myself very well. Yet it was terrifying to put aside those false images and take a clear look at myself—I simply didn't know what I would find.

My favorite mask was People-pleaser. Hiding behind it, I could easily relate to others' masks, such as Authority Figure, Pollyanna, or Poor Pitiful Me. As People-pleaser, I was often comparing myself with others, putting them above or below me in value.

When I put people below me, I could play the role of Helper or Rescuer. When I put them above me, I could play Victim or Helpless Child. Stuck in those roles, dealing with each other mask-to-mask (not face-to-face), we could never get to know each other.

Many develop their egos around their jobs, or their place in a family. They assume that their true selves are wrapped up in being "a successful doctor" or "a good mother." Those images affect their daily decisions. They work hard to keep those masks in place.

As a minister's wife, I know there are certain things expected of that role. In fact, I began my "career" with a strong image of what that meant. I also take pride in my role as mother of three daughters. But there is no guarantee that any of these roles will be permanent. Illness or death could strip them from me in a hurry. How tragic it would be if I had no other identity! I balanced my various responsibilities nicely, but apart from the masks I wore, who was I really?

I began hearing my friends who were in recovery programs talk about "ego-slaying." Frankly, I was anxious about that term. It called up too many memories of old-time revivalists urging sinners to "become nothing" in the eyes of God. I didn't want to become nothing. I was already afraid that, after God finished stripping off my masks, there would be nothing there. Others would violate my boundaries and take over my life, making all my decisions for me.

I had spent a lifetime constructing that ego of mine. It would not die easily. So I clung to my ego, my self-sufficiency, my arrogance, my pride.

But God kept showing me the dangers of clinging to those masks. Our egos can isolate and alienate us from each other. We become judgmental and critical—if we sand down this part and tack on another part, maybe we can change each other enough to be happy together on this planet. Our egos assure us that someone else is to blame for everything that's wrong. There must be a scapegoat somewhere. Presumably we will all have peace again if we can just identify the culprit and deal with him.

Sometimes we get stuck in a role or a stage of life. Mothers who have lived through their children are frustrated (and frustrate others!) when they don't move out of their mother role when the primary parenting years are over.

Personality types can become stuck, too, in a rigid ego state. "I just can't change" is the response of an authority figure who doesn't want to bend (and may think he cannot). "This is just the way I am" is the battle cry of a person fixed in irresponsibility and stuck in a child's ego. "This always happens to me; I'm doomed" is the wail of a victim, committed to that image.

While I am a proponent of support groups for recovery from all kinds of addictions and dysfunctions, and while I have found the Twelve Steps to be vital to my own growth, I hold a concern that seeing myself *only* as a co-dependent can inhibit my becoming all that God created me to be. Getting stuck on one part of my personality or deifying my character defect (and then expecting others to relate to that part) is one of the ego's ways of keeping me isolated from others.

As I prayed, and listened in prayer, one "John the Baptist" experience after another rolled over me, calling me to repent of these attitudes, preparing the way for Christ's healing presence. I began to wonder what it would take to get us human beings to come out from our hiding places and be truly open to each other.

What would it take for me to become a free agent, responsible and loving, willing to give up fear and self-will in order for the will of God to be released? What would it take for me to learn how to submit without the fear of being consumed or controlled? I began to see that my very survival depended on coming out of hiding and learning how to get along. I would learn much as I plowed and slogged my way through this new challenge in my prayer life.

Sometimes God allows me to take my lessons in situations outside my own relationships. I think He does this because He knows we can bear only so much schooling at one time! In one child who often visited our home, I got a good look at the little child in me.

Mindy was a lovely child, well-dressed and with impeccable manners. There was something about her that tugged at me, however. When I addressed her, she would face me almost as if I were a high-ranking officer in a military squadron. "Yes, ma'am" and "No, ma'am," she would say, precisely at the right times, giving me the impression that she was going to do whatever I wanted. Later, however, I would notice that she had done exactly as *she* chose, disregarding whatever instructions I had given.

That is the way ego works: *It gives the appearance of one reality, all the time hiding the real truth behind a carefully constructed mask.* I saw in Mindy the early stages of ego-building. The primary purpose was protection.

Though this child had a sophistication beyond her years and operated with unusual poise, her eyes were the eyes of one who has learned to watch for danger. When she was visiting in our home, I would suddenly become aware that she was watching me, the "authority figure," scrutinizing my face for messages she would then interpret to keep herself safe.

Mindy's young, bright eyes darted back and forth, always scanning her environment. She was ever watchful for a door of escape, betraying the wounded inner child who had seen too much of life's raw edges. Whenever I looked into those young eyes, I saw a highly developed fear, and I grieved for what was to come for this child who had already learned to hide behind a mask of composure.

Mindy, like all of us to one degree or another, is set up for trouble in relationships, for already she has constructed barriers and walls. Already she has decided that it isn't safe to be close to folks, that only shrewd adaptation can protect her. With a child's keen abilities to observe, but immature abilities to interpret that which is observed, Mindy has designed for herself a persona to present to the world in order to survive.

Mindy bothered me because she held up a mirror in which I saw my own reflection. Although my growing up was in the context of a safe and nurturing environment, still, I learned early to present myself in such a way as to be accepted by those I loved.

Early on, I learned to conform to others' expectations, hiding my thoughts and stuffing my real feelings way down deep. Quickly, I caught on to the idea that "good little girls" keep themselves out of trouble and behave, or at least give the appearance that they are behaving! People who don't make waves and stay out of the way don't get hurt. Those who work at getting along get along. In a common human tendency, my real self went into hiding.

Developing an ego, that part of self that the world sees, is a natural part of growing up in a world that demands certain behaviors. My ego was formed unconsciously and in the ways typical to children, who are helpless and vulnerable, as I emerged from childhood through youth and into adulthood. It was formed in response to external stimuli.

While ego is a necessary part of self-identity, at some point in life it begins to keep us from being honest with others. The ego that served a useful purpose in the formative years of your personality starts to work against you. When you get serious about spiritual growth and praying, you will find yourself battling your ego.

Ego puts up a huge fight to stay in charge. Left alone, the facade, the false self, becomes rigid and unbending. In my case, my ego convinces me that I could control myself and others. It makes me think that I am right and that I must have my own way. Sadly, in a distortion of "let your conscience be your guide," ego makes me think it is the voice of God, and that is why I need to be accountable to others on the journey who know my real self.

That duplicitous ego tells me lies about myself, telling me what I can and can't do, *based on a shame-based concept of who I am*. It beats me up with the "shoulds" and "oughts" about life. Most of all, that ego tells me in loud and obnoxious tones about limitation. It makes me limit God and, in some ways, it limits my own abilities. Ego leads me to idealize others, focusing on their giftedness instead of claiming and exercising my own.

57

Ego makes me take on too much, insisting that I work harder and longer and with greater intensity than is humanly possible. Ego tempts me constantly to be more to others than a human is called to be. Without a clear sense of my limitations in strength and ability, which come through prayer, I violate my own physical self trying to do too much.

"You had better be able to deliver what you promise," a long-time friend said to me one day. She had come home to San Angelo for some quality time with me, but I was much too busy with all my new friends in our young church to spend that time with her. In a painful confrontation, she commented on my ability to "work a crowd," never missing a cue, performing as I had come to expect myself to perform. "You are so friendly that people think you want to be friends, but you can't possibly be close to that many people." My People-pleaser self was a hiding place, a mask behind which I could retreat.

Being the enlightened person that I was, I immediately moved into a posture of defending myself. The thing I most wanted to hide from her was the fact that she had uncovered what I had suspected in myself all along—that I was really a phony. That was a piece of information I could barely allow into my own awareness, and the possibility of someone else's seeing it was enough to send me into a panic-stricken (and therefore angry) defense of myself.

Those words stung me for years before I fully understood the implications of her wisdom. I thought she simply didn't understand the demands of my job or the strengths of my personality. After all, didn't others praise my ability to work with others? Didn't they talk about what a great "people person" I was?

Little did I know that my abilities as a people person and my rather intensive training in this had begun to work against me. In what Anne Wilson Schaef calls an "escape from intimacy," I had learned to make quick connections, to relate deeply in a hurry and then make an exit before things became too complicated. Waking up out of my darkness, I came upon the stark reality that I had a multitude of acquaintances, but very few close friends. Even worse, I had convinced myself that I liked things that way *because it was safer*. (There's that scared little girl again!)

The only problem was that I was missing out on the nurturing and closeness that human beings desperately need. Because of my mistaken notions and the promptings of my ego, I was depriving myself of that secure sense of belonging by keeping significant people at arms' distance. I had complained that others didn't want to be close, but within the disciplines of meditation, I was brought to the truth about myself—*I* was scared to be close.

Another insidious problem created by the ego is that it makes me think my problems belong to someone else. The ego can't bear to let your real self tell the truth about your own character flaws, and so it casts the beams of accusations outward.

As I kept on practicing relational prayer, God opened my eyes to see, through the torture of broken relationships and frustrated closeness, how this projection keeps me at odds with others. It suddenly began to dawn on me that the darkness I was seeing in others was merely a reflection of what I didn't like in myself. To my fascination, I recognized that my ability to ferret out others' faults and to home in on others' ugly feelings was simply my way to avoid looking honestly in the mirror. The chaos I was causing on the outside was a reflection of the chaos within me. The culprit was that old ego, fighting to stay alive and to keep me from discovering the power of the presence of God within my life.

In order to maintain this false self, you have to "stuff" true feelings and put on the face that you want the world to see. Stuffing feelings is a common trait of people-pleasers, and it is a primary form of dishonesty. Denying feelings is one way of staying stuck in the darkness.

There is a small scar over my eye that reminds me each day of my tendency to stuff my feelings and "perform" according to my ego's specifications. One day, I was getting dressed for a consultation with the director of juvenile services in San Angelo. I had been called in to discuss the runaway child of a friend, and I was more than a little uptight about the encounter. I did not want to go to this interview, but neither did I want to disappoint my friend. I was actually angry about being drawn into the problem, but out of habit I stuffed my anger.

I carefully put on my makeup and dressed for the day. When I walked back into my bedroom, I tripped on the bedspread and fell, hitting my eye on the corner of a metal bookcase. Stunned, I extricated myself from the awkward position, holding my hand up to my head, which was splitting with pain. To put it mildly, I was seeing stars!

My first awareness was that blood was coursing down my face, and the very next thoughts were about cleaning myself up so that I would look "right" for my interview. I carefully reapplied my makeup and went to my interview, discreetly dabbing my eye with a tissue, hoping the interviewer would not ask me why my eye was bleeding!

It's not a superhuman quality to go on with the show, I realize. Others go on about their business when they don't feel like it or when they'd rather be doing "power lounging"! In this case, however, the scar over my eye reminds me how easily I lie to myself about what I am feeling. It is a daily flag, warning me to tell the truth to myself about my inner kingdom.

Pride wouldn't let me stay home and take care of myself, nor would it let me admit that I was in pain. That stuffing of feelings is a self-defeating habit that thwarts the sharing of the splendor of Christ's grace.

Ego was a haven of dark grandiosity, where I could retreat to tell myself how others had imposed on me and what terrific and unusual pressures life had placed upon me. Ego created the opposite of what I wanted, a life of serenity and intimacy, because it Erased God Out of my consciousness. In a perverse way, ego becomes a substitute for God, destroying or at least impeding the possibilities of surrender.

I would like to declare that my prayer life dramatically and instantaneously transformed my relationships with others into models of harmony and peace. The truth is that, for a time, the more I worked at allowing Christ to be the center of my relationships, the greater difficulty I had in getting along with others. For a period of time that seemed endless, my relationships were just getting worse. The old ways would not simply die, but would shake the very life out of me before they finally let go.

It was as if the mere desire to walk in the light unleashed all the forces of darkness. I was appalled—and continue to be—at the resistance to loving and being loved that I can generate.

Slowly, sometimes imperceptibly, I began to come out of the darkness and into the light. As I continued affirming the reality of the presence of Christ within me, I began to get hints of the splendor that was to come. I began to know without a doubt that only Christ's love can generate that healing fire among us. Only the love of Christ can melt the masks and bring down the walls between us. Only Christ can bring us true peace.

The pain of my relationships prepared the way for restoration. As I continued to follow the promptings of the Spirit, I was led to healing pools. I began to trust myself and the Voice of God within me, and then I began to trust others.

As Christ joined me in my journey and opened my eyes, I found that I was journeying into depths of myself I never dreamed existed. Encouraged to face my own brokenness and inadequacies, I also was confronted with the complete adequacy of God. Thus my relationships have become the very instruments of grace and growth that I need, and each conflict has become a teacher, a guide, or even a healer. In meeting others openly, honestly, and freely, I have met God.

Indeed, Christ initiates the healing of our inner selves through the encounters we have with each other. As He mediates among us in ways that are sometimes complicated and painful, He restores and reconciles us. In drawing us into His presence, He brings us closer to each other, whittling away our false selves so that we can relate true self to true self.

It was when the two disciples from the Emmaus Road *broke bread* with Christ that their eyes were opened. If I am to find healing and if I am to see, I must continue to partake of the broken bread. That is, I must continue to return to the presence of Christ.

On a recent evening, the telephone rang right at dinnertime. With three teenagers in our home and with the demands of our respective ministries, the phone is always a *force*.

The caller would not give her name, but she did tell me at the outset that she was "chemically unbalanced" and that she wanted to talk about her problems to Martus. However, since he wasn't there, I would do. So she launched into a detailed account of her life.

I sat there, torn between the needs of my family and the needs of this unnamed stranger. Which voice would I follow? Would I play the role and pretend I was interested when I really wasn't? Would I try to work up compassion because I was "supposed to"? How would letting this woman take my precious family time be of help to her when, in the morning's sobriety, she wouldn't even remember our conversation?

As I carried on my internal debate, my children were swarming around me, hungry and impatient with this interruption. I started to tell the caller my predicament, when she hooked my pride and my ego. "I've read your book," she said, "and you seem to be a spiritual, caring person."

I was hooked. Would I allow her to use me and abuse my time so that I could maintain my image with her? Would I neglect my own children to satisfy my ego's need to be a helper? Would I tell the truth or would I lie?

Each day, I confront my ego and its insatiable demands. Each day, I must choose, and while there is grace in the midst of the choosing, I can never take for granted that I am "totally surrendered" to Christ's love.

The Spirit of Christ continues to bring challenges. He continues to reveal truth, and He continues to bring my true self (that He created) out of hiding, so that I can be an effective instrument. But it doesn't happen overnight.

5
Boundaries for Freedom

Be firm without being forceful, say no without walling off, and be self-respecting while still respecting the rights of others.

—Maria Arapakis

Put on the new man which was created according to God, in righteousness and true holiness.

Ephesians 4:24 NKJV

———————◆———————

It was a balmy fall afternoon and I was finishing the last mile of my walk. Suddenly, as I rounded the corner onto Oak Mountain, the Voice spoke in my head.

"You can't serve two masters, Jeanie," It said, and I was so startled that I looked around me to see if someone had joined me. And then I heard the words again: "You can't serve two masters."

No one had to tell me, this time, who was speaking. Long years of listening make me know more easily when it is God's Voice and when it is one of my own voices, though I continue to check out my impressions with others, and with Scripture.

On that afternoon, I didn't have to ask anyone what that meant, for the experiences in prayer had prepared the way for me. I knew that I let other things and other people take the position in my life that only God Himself could fill. Nor did I need to spend a great deal of time figuring out who the other masters were. I needed only to admit that I let others play God to me. God has had to work long and hard to help me erect appropriate boundaries for myself.

When ego begins to go, it is inappropriate and dangerous to be standing emotionally naked before the world. God intends for us to have personal boundaries to take the place of the walls and masks and fortresses, but it takes work, prayer, and practice to negotiate those boundaries.

As I continued to give priority to the Lordship of Christ, I discovered that there were too many masters for me to name, tyrants and slave drivers of my own making that had been allowed to set my agenda. The truth is that I am prone to allow others' whims, moods, and agendas, both hidden and overt, determine how I feel and think and act.

The way these other masters work is cunning and insidious, and all tied up with the image I have of myself as a "good" person. Without the constant and careful vigilance of prayer, I can even convince myself that what I am doing is right. Indeed, it is still too easy for me to get the Voice of God mixed up with the voices of others. The growth edge for me is a constant minding of my personal boundaries.

For example, left to my natural self, I can be feeling perfectly fine, but if someone in a dour mood comes into my presence, it is as if there are no boundaries between that person and me. In a perversion of my natural sensitivity, I can reach out with my emotional skin, scoop up the other's feelings, and take them on as my own.

"You must have appropriate boundaries," Keith Miller was saying from the podium. Our church was sponsoring a Singles' Conference, and Keith had the audience spellbound. He was speaking truth in ways that profoundly defined both the problem and the solution. His work with Pia Mellody, a leading authority on co-dependency, had changed his life, and he was passing his experience on to us as a light for our pathways.

Boundaries! I had heard the term for months now, but suddenly I was teachable. *Boundaries* are limits, indeed, but they also indicate protection and responsibility. *Boundaries* indicate individuality and personal freedom. I saw now how the work of the previous months had prepared the way for this new state of awareness and understanding.

Later, as I pondered the concept of boundaries, I recalled my mother's admonitions when I was a child about "playing in my own backyard." I had the freedom and the privilege to do just about whatever I wanted *within the confines of my own space*. We didn't have a fence around our backyard, but I knew exactly where the boundaries were.

Having good boundaries means that I know where I end and you begin. I know the difference between my responsibilities and yours. I let you into my space *when I choose to do so* and I respect your physical and emotional space. In other words, I don't run over into your backyard and start rearranging it, because that is *your* space and I am to respect it.

As Melody Beattie says in her book, *Co-Dependent No More*, "I can develop boundaries, limits that say, 'This is as far as I'll go,' and 'This is what I won't tolerate.' " I was to learn that the Spirit of Christ will help me to say no where I need to. Even more exciting to me is the freedom to say yes to new adventures and new levels of intimacy with others.

I have learned that good boundaries permit me to listen to another person's viewpoint without having to change mine or adopt his. I have a right to my own thoughts, opinions, and biases. I can also choose to change my mind. I can also allow another person to hold a different point of view without feeling that one of us has to be "right" or "wrong." Having good internal boundaries means that I am free to allow and tolerate difference.

Having good boundaries means that others can't make me feel guilty, angry, or ashamed. It also means that I don't try to control others' feelings. Good boundaries keep me from duping myself into thinking I have power over what others are feeling.

Good boundaries allow me to let others have their pain and to walk through their dark valleys and not get sucked under with them. When my boundaries are in place, I know the difference between my "stuff," or my emotional baggage, and your stuff. I can have empathy with you, but I don't have to take on your suffering.

I shall never forget the day I discovered that I act out others' feelings. It was a watershed moment for me. It was one of those liberating experiences that forever changed my perceptions. While I don't always see the situations coming in time to avoid acting out another's anger or fear, I am getting better.

"Do you act out others' anger?" my perceptive friend asked.

At first, in the silence, my ego tried to keep me from knowing the truth because it would mean change. Knowing the truth would also mean that others would have to change as well, and I had a long history of protecting others from looking bad.

"You seem to be the one who walks around with egg on your face," she continued, "while the one who is *really* angry doesn't ever have to deal with it! Why do you do others' emotional work for them?"

I was stunned, but when I walked out of the building that day, the sun was shining more brightly than before. From that day forward, even with many lapses, I have moved toward identifying the times when others are angry, fearful, or *whatever*, and then detaching myself from their emotions and letting them deal with their own baggage.

Recently, I allowed myself to become very upset about the behavior of a member of one of my groups. She had abused her group privileges over and over, and in the process had hurt the group members. In trying to "protect" the group, I took on her responsibilities and explained away her behavior to the other group members.

After a particularly upsetting group session, another member of the group called me and quietly told me that she had a rule that *no one outside her family* had the privilege of evoking the strong feelings I expressed in the group. In a sweet and respectful way, my "student" let me know that I needed to practice what I was teaching. I became Exhibit A in the study of proper boundaries.

The reality is that because I am sensitive and perceptive, I do have the ability to empathize. It hardly matters whether or not I have had the actual experience you have had; if you want someone to suffer with you, come on over. I have lots of practice at feeling others' pain.

Through consistent prayer and meditation, God began to reveal how the gift of empathy had begun to turn sour for me and work against me. My strength had become my weakness, so that I couldn't be of real help to others because I got trapped in their pain. My feelings would clog my brain so that I couldn't see clearly. Meditation was the key for discovering this distortion of a natural gift.

Having good boundaries means that I own my own time. I am learning that I am to answer to God Himself for the use of my time. For too many days of my life, I have waited around to see what others would do with their time, and then I would decide how I would spend my time. I would allow any needy stranger to consume my time, draining me of emotional reserves and keeping me from accomplishing what I needed to accomplish for that day. Then, I would be furious at the people who needed me most, my children and husband, because others had used me up.

There's a twist to this. I always professed to be "available" to those who needed me. This image that I tried to present kept me stuck. When the light finally began to dawn in my head, I saw that I was neglecting God's call on the day's work. I was tyrannized by the urgent, to the neglect of the important.

In prayer, I began to see that I had been given stewardship over my time, my resources, and my energy. I began to feel a tug to commit all of these to Christ, confessing my tendencies to let others take that place of master and asking God to show me how to set proper boundaries. The amazing thing is that when I do what I am supposed to do and follow the real Master, I am free to say "Yes!" to the things He has in mind for me. Meditation and practicing the presence of Christ are terrific time-savers.

Good boundaries mean that I allow others to make it or break it on their own. I discovered that I was avoiding living my own life by taking on Martus's or my children's successes or failures as my own. I thought it was up to me to make sure that they made it. Without appropriate boundaries, I set myself up to feel bad if they failed. Any trouble they had, I figured, was always my fault. However, if they succeeded, *it was in spite of me!* What a trap I set for myself.

The up side of this tendency is that I am a great team player and I can be vitally interested in the details of your projects. If you want someone to hear about the ins and outs of what you are doing, I'm available. I am fascinated by people's stories.

As I continued to practice relational prayer, however, I realized I was meddling in my loved ones' affairs. Being the sensitive, perceptive person that I am, I picked up on this when my children or husband told me to back off!

Invariably, my feelings were hurt. Equally predictable was the way they began withholding information from me *because of my reactions to what they would tell me.* I couldn't figure out what problems were theirs to solve and what were mine. As often as not, I would spend more time twisting around in their business *to keep from having to face what was my business!*

It was "safer," my ego told me, to focus on their endeavors and their business, which I thought I could help, than it was to face my own business, which I knew I was absolutely powerless to change. Again, the image of myself as Helper was part of that ego that had to go. Only then could I be of real help as an effective instrument, tuned to God's promptings.

What I thought was being interested in their pursuits was being perceived as violating their boundaries. To my shock and horror, I realized that others thought I was interfering and controlling. Not only was I unable to keep others' stuff out of my own life, I didn't know how to stay out of others' business!

"You need good boundaries," Keith Miller kept saying, "if you are going to be a true disciple of Christ." Indeed, I was hearing about boundaries everywhere I turned. It seemed that all the books I was reading eventually got around to the issue of boundaries.

My consciousness about boundaries brought up a memory that had troubled me for years. A much older, wiser friend was horrified by the way others would use me. It bothered her that I allowed others to meddle in what wasn't their business or say harshly critical things. I, on the other hand, somehow thought I had to take whatever people dished out. That was, after all, the only way I could "keep the peace."

"There's something about you," Mrs. Hughes told me, shaking her head, "that needs to set some limits. You need to put some dignity up around you so that other people won't say such hurtful things to you." Mrs. Hughes was ahead of her time. She knew about boundaries.

As I continued searching, I was led to the conviction that establishing good boundaries had a great deal to do with keeping the first commandment: "You shall not have any other gods before Me." The more deeply I went into meditation, the more

70

clear it became to me that I was serving numerous masters, empowering mere mortals with god-like dominion over me.

Establishing boundaries is one of the practical benefits of practicing the presence of Christ. When Christ's presence is part of our daily events, truth is also present, revealing where our actions must change.

Establishing boundaries makes it unnecessary to build walls between people who love each other. It also frees me to deal with the feelings I tend to stuff deep inside myself when I am trying to live through others or am controlled by others.

Prayer, then, sweeps out the channels between us with its masterful broom of truth, making a space in which grace and peace can reside.

The process of "ego-slaying" must include, then, the building of an adequate boundary system. Maintaining conscious contact with God both leads to this process and facilitates it. That process continues in the context of daily living. Building boundaries is a whole lot like waking up, as if from a deep coma. It is about becoming conscious and aware, about acting instead of reacting. It is about moving from need-love to gift-love.

Merely learning about boundaries didn't create them, and I learned that establishing appropriate limits would be as difficult as the ego-slaying. Being born into a new way of thinking and living was a treacherous journey, but one empowered by the Spirit of Life. I was to learn the meaning of Jesus' statement, "I am the Way," as He took the individual challenges of my days and revealed the way of setting boundaries bit by bit.

Again, as I began to set boundaries, my ego's old ways kicked in. I identified ways in which I substituted information and skill for intimacy, hiding behind my knowledge. None of that could free my heart from its fear. As the distance between what I knew to do and what I actually did became greater, my guilt also grew. I should be perfect, shouldn't I?

Setting boundaries about time and money and space felt strange because I was so unaccustomed to autonomy. Even now, setting boundaries sometimes makes me feel I am being selfish, and so I must continually surrender my will to God.

Healing always begins for me when I trust God to set the boundaries. When I come to the end of my ability before God, then He meets me at the point of my need to show me each step. God is in charge of my healing, and I must count on Him to accomplish the task of restoring me. I am utterly dependent on Him. Every day, I must seek God's guidance in my use of time and the conducting of my affairs.

In a noisy restaurant with my soul friend, I finally understood the humility necessary for boundaries. I had given her excuses and lines for years about my excesses. Finally, on that day, she forced my hand and made me tell the truth about how I "enjoyed" letting others play God in my life.

Sitting there in the protection of the public noise, it felt as if my outer shell were crumbling, and for a moment, I was mortified. Who would I be, I wondered, if I took charge of my own life? What would I do in relationships if I began to be responsible and autonomous? What would *others* do if I began seeking God's will before theirs?

Gently, as always, Sandra began painting word pictures of what kind of joys I might experience if I let God take control of my will. She described the real intimacy that is possible between two adult individuals who are willing to live in freedom instead of a tangled state.

After lunch, I clutched my coat around me and walked out into the biting winter wind. I felt as though I had been pushed and shoved out of my protective shell into a new land. I knew that part of me had died, and I prayed that it was the false self that could love only with a limited heart. I prayed that this wrenching pain was a birth process, a beginning.

72

Driving home, I could see how God had been leading me up to this moment through all the months of practicing the discipline of prayer. I knew that it was because of His guidance that Sandra had known how to confront me and that I had suddenly had the courage to face the truth about myself.

That was good enough news to me, but even better was the realization that, instead of being ashamed about the contents of my heart and head, I felt liberated and cleansed. Furthermore, I no longer felt the need to rush myself to change. I knew that the process of a changed heart would evolve over my entire lifetime and that the fruition of that day's work would come in the fullness of time—as surely as the barren trees would, in their time, produce the leaves of springtime.

I saw my broken self clearly that day, but the real gift was that I got a glimpse of the individual self God wanted me to be, in relation to others. I also saw that, if I wanted to continue to walk in the light, I had to be both patient and firm with myself. The presence of Christ had indeed opened me up to my real self and to my potential, but if I was to continue in the ways of love, I had to guard carefully my times of prayer and devotion.

God has to break down those dividing walls within the individual heart so that He can break down the dividing walls between us. In my case, He had to show me that He could not do through me what I would not let Him do in me. Sandra told me later that I had had one of the big lessons in humility, the lesson of learning my need for God.

Humility keeps me remembering that I depend on God for the protective boundaries I need. I count on Him to warn me when I begin putting up walls again. I must rely on God's Spirit to go before me, so that I will not be afraid, and to follow behind me, so that I can let go of what has been.

I will probably always struggle with people-pleasing, just as others fight with their people-avoiding habits. I will probably continue to look to others for affirmation; after all, people have smiles I can see and pats of approval I can feel. I trust God enough, however, to know that He will always bring me back to the only place where I find ultimate worth and meaning.

"She thinks you are cold," someone told me only last week. This time last year, I would have reacted with horror that someone didn't perceive the loving, tender person I really am. Only a year ago, those very words would have sent me into a dither of people-pleasing. I would have knocked myself out to redeem my image in that person's eyes, striving to prove her wrong.

It felt good to receive the words of another and yet not engage with them. It felt good to step back from the criticism, detaching from the judgment, and hearing the feelings of the offended party. I could, thank God, sense her pain and not react to it. As I have changed and have built boundaries for myself instead of walls, others have perceived the changes in terms of their own needs, but I am not responsible for that.

For too much of my life, I have stuck my neck in the yokes of others' demands and needs, nearly breaking my neck, trying to please. Too easily, I have forgotten the primacy of Christ's call. That Carpenter, legend has it, made yokes that fit perfectly and did not chafe.

Setting appropriate boundaries doesn't mean that I neglect others or that I just "do my own thing." In fact, setting boundaries means that I am able to love with a higher quality of love, a love that grows out of a healthy self-love and self-respect that originates in the heart of a loving, gracious Father.

In a moment of sweetness last month, I chose to extend love and nurture to Martus as he walked through a difficult time within our church family. As I listened to him pour out his worries and fears, I made a decision to be strong and to "sit steady in the boat," as my father had tried to teach me.

"I know I will lapse," I related to Martus, wanting to let him know that I might let my boundaries slip. "But I am declaring to you that I will not stay in that lapse, for I have decided to live in peace and to love without fear, even if there are unhappy church members."

When I am centered in the Father's love, I am not so easily thrown off course by others' deeds and attitudes. I love out of an inner wellspring that isn't dependent on what others do or don't do. When I take the time to put myself in the position to receive God's love, I am able to love from the inside out in gift-love.

In allowing God to meet my needs and in trusting that He is meeting them (even though I cannot at the moment see how He is doing it), I am able to love without unnecessary concern for the worries and details of daily life.

God used Scripture to teach me a lesson about boundaries. I was working with a spiritual director who asked me to think about what Scripture fit my current growth challenges. Much to my shock, the story of the Samaritan woman at the well popped into my head.

Not that one! I hurriedly told myself. *I'll think of another story that fits me. I don't have anything in common with that wanton woman, for goodness' sake!*

No matter how hard I tried, however, the Samaritan woman stayed in my mind. I remembered my embarrassment at telling this spiritual director which story had chosen me; I also remember the surprise on her face. Even now, I chuckle to think what she must have thought!

I hoped she would tell me to look for another story, but, since she trusted the way God's Spirit quickens the memory, she insisted that I continue with that Samaritan woman. All the way home, then, I wrestled with that Scripture. In a quiet moment of prayer, I realized that God had brought the Samaritan woman to my awareness in order to teach me about myself.

The Samaritan woman didn't have good boundaries either.

She was probably a people-pleaser like me, and perhaps a co-dependent, for she had given herself away to five different husbands. She, like me, had looked outside herself for meaning and purpose. She, like me, had given her inner kingdom to other folks, letting them determine her worth and value.

Meditating on that Scripture, I worked with the story in my prayer time, seeing myself standing there with the Samaritan woman and Jesus at the well. I imagined what she would tell me about herself and about me. I was able to get inside her skin and feel what it was like to be in her shoes. In the process of praying the Scriptures in that manner, I made discoveries that proved to be life-changing.

The Samaritan woman and I had something else in common. Each of us discovered that the only permanent source of life is in Christ. Jesus Christ is the only One who can fill up the empty buckets of our lives. He is the only One who can give that sense of inner security and serenity that makes love possible.

Jesus Christ is the only Lover who is constant and unfailing. His is the only love that is unconditional. When I regularly meet Him at the well, He gives me all I need to love others for Him. When I keep my regular appointment with Christ, He frees me to love as He intended me to love.

There is another gift of that divine appointment. Jesus Christ consistently clothes me with His armor, as Paul describes in Ephesians 6:10–17. He gives me the protection of His truth and righteousness. He puts me in the sandals of peace, gives me the shield of faith, the helmet of salvation, and the sword of the Spirit—the Word of God. That is the best boundary of all.

6
Instruments of His Peace

I have discovered no way in which I can separate my prayer
life from my practice of caring for others. . . . It is difficult
to understand genuine, self-giving love without some experience of the love of God and the prayer and meditation
which so often lead to that experience.

—Morton Kelsey

"Peter, do you love me?" Jesus said to him a third time.
"You know I love you, Lord," Peter responded. "Then feed
my sheep," Jesus said.

John 21:17 AT

———❧———

There's a dream I can't seem to give up. My dream centers
around being involved with a group of people who are willing to
be all that God intended them to be. Each of us within this group
would get his identity from God instead of looking to roles and
images to give us worth and meaning. All of us would be in touch
with our gifts and willing to take responsibility for using those
gifts to declare the love of God.

In my dream, each person would know his or her mission on
this earth. Just as a corporation declares a mission statement,
each person would declare what he was to do with his giftedness.
In a kind of holy stewardship, each would take seriously the call
of God.

This dream seems to be most practical to me. With as much need as there is in the world, it seems obvious that every person's gifts and energy are needed. Surely, if each person were doing what he was supposed to be doing, the problems of the world could be solved, or at least we could make some progress in that direction.

Sometimes, I try to be more "realistic," which means I try to see things from the point of view of a typical world citizen. After all, there is great evidence that points to the depravity of man. There is a lot to keep me discouraged. However, the more I practice the presence of Love, the more I yearn for my vision to become a reality.

I hold on to my dream because I keep seeing people transformed by practicing the presence of Christ. Through my work in spiritual direction and in leading spiritual growth groups, I see people make the shift from being consumed with their own pain to being willing to reach out to others. As individuals continue practicing Christ's presence, they move away from a self-centeredness to genuine compassion for others. The warmth of Christ's presence stirs something in hearts that have been shut down by fear and coldness.

I have seen people come in the doors of the Growth Options office who don't believe there is anything of worth in their lives. Because of hurtful things that were done to them, they have assumed a victim role and are stuck in what others have done to them. Through prayer and through interaction with others, they begin to move out of that victim stance and start doing for others. In the process of giving, they receive.

As we practice the presence of Christ between us, each of us gains new courage in giving up that distorted self-image and taking on the image Christ intends. In that presence, it is possible to move beyond the victim posture and see oneself as whole, responsible, and mature. The presence of Christ through prayer

heals a reactive style of living and makes it possible to live pro-
actively.

I'll never forget the day, years ago, when I prayed that God
would "use" me as an instrument of His peace. Throughout my
youth and early adulthood, I was afraid to pray that prayer. I
didn't particularly want to be a missionary, and I certainly didn't
want to be known as a "fanatic." In those early years of my
spiritual quest, I didn't have a clear sense of who I was or how
God might use me. And who did I think I was, to expect that God
could use me or would even want to!

However, on the day I reported for duty, I had come to the
place in my own spiritual journey of wanting to be used by God.
Somehow, I had matured to the place of knowing that God's
ways of using us are consistent with our giftedness. In other
words, I didn't know how God would use me, but I was pretty
sure He wouldn't send me to Africa to be an accountant!

I had come to love the famous prayer of Saint Francis of Assissi
and had prayed it many times as an example of a "pretty prayer."

> *Lord, make me an instrument of Thy peace;*
> *Where there is hatred, let me sow love;*
> *Where there is doubt, faith;*
> *Where there is darkness, light;*
> *and where there is sadness, joy.*
>
> *O, Divine Master, grant that I may*
> *not so much seek to be consoled as to console;*
> *to be understood, as to understand;*
> *to be loved, as to love;*
>
> *For it is in giving that we receive,*
> *   it is in pardoning that we are pardoned,*
> *and it is in dying that we are born*
> *   to eternal life.*

I really believed with my head that the way to real wholeness was in letting God use me to communicate His love and grace. At this point in my journey, I know that truth with my *heart*.

Finally, one cold, sunny day in midwinter, I prayed a fervent prayer of commitment to God, wondering if He could possibly use someone like me. I had no idea what all was involved in being an instrument of God's peace, but I was willing.

I had grown up hearing the phrases "blessed to be a blessing" and "saved to serve." What that meant for my individual life, I did not know initially, but my willingness to know opened all sorts of doors. In the process of these last years, I have learned that it is in being an instrument of healing that I am healed. Saint Francis was right. It is in giving that we receive.

The whole process of being instruments of Christ is a fascinating study in cooperative effort. It seems that God leads me out to be His instrument, and in that venture, I discover all sorts of broken places in my own life. Then, as I turn those places over to His healing touch, He brings other circumstances and experiences and people to test out the area of healing He is trying to accomplish in my life.

Through the years, I have turned again and again to Scripture as guidance for the journey. The Bible is a touchstone of power for me. In the adventure of grace, Scripture gives objective truth to the experiences I have had. Through meditating on the passages, God teaches me exactly what I need to know at each phase and the Living Word comes to me through the written Word.

God often uses interesting instruments to convey His message. Maintaining a continuous prayer life keeps the channels of communication open so that I can recognize that message when it comes.

Recently, God selected some elementary school children in our church to bring home to me a special truth. As a part of the

children's sermon one bright fall morning, several children re-
enacted the story of the Good Samaritan for proud parents. For
me, they unwittingly revealed a message from Christ which I
needed.

The process had actually started weeks before the Sunday
morning drama. One day, after working with my sponsor on a
thorny issue in a relationship, I left her house with a kind of
amazement at how she always knew exactly where to direct my
attention. I could so easily trap myself, going around in circles
with what I thought was the problem, or I could get stuck doing
the same wrong thing over and over. Because of her wisdom and
sensitivity, however, she always knew exactly the place that
needed attention.

As I drove home, the story of the Good Samaritan bubbled up
in my mind. As I have learned to do, I paused in my mental
wanderings to pay attention to what had appeared spontaneously
in my mind's eye. What, I wondered, was there for me in this
story? What would I discover as I meditated on that Scripture
passage?

I got out my Bible as soon as I returned home and read the
passage. I mulled it over and over in my mind, identifying with
the different characters, visualizing myself in their shoes, trying
to feel what they must have felt. The more I pondered the story,
however, the more I came up with the same truths I had heard
all my life.

Finally, I got out the commentaries to see if there was something new I could discover in them. What was there was interesting, but it wasn't anything I didn't already know. Perhaps I had
"juiced" that story enough, I thought, and so I put the story on
the back burner of my mind, trusting the Spirit of God to bring
to my mind whatever He wanted me to know at the appropriate

time. For several days thereafter, the story would reemerge in my conscious thoughts, but still there were no flashes of insight.

God was to wait, drawing me deeper and deeper into exploring the story, before He made His big points. He was to make a holy space of encounter between myself and His Spirit as I sat in our darkened worship center and watched the children play out their parts.

The villains did their thing with gusto, and the priest and Levite amused us with their self-righteousness. I couldn't keep from thinking about how easily these television veterans acted out the violence. It wasn't quite so funny, however, that they could portray apathy and disgust toward a wounded person. Where had they learned such insensitivity?

What a relief I felt when the Good Samaritan came on the scene and knew how to portray compassion! As I watched this young child act out such tenderness and humility toward the injured man, the message of that parable suddenly hit me. The weeks of meditating on that Scripture came to me through youthful instruments.

That's what Sandra's been doing! The words thundered in my head. *And that is exactly what we are to do with each other.* I saw that Sandra had been God's instrument of healing for me, applying the oil of grace to my wounds, and her wounds had become medicine for me! While we may not actually come upon a wounded victim on the side of the road, wounded people cross our pathways every single day.

The truth for me was that Sandra had given me great advice through the years, both from her knowledge and her experience. She had, again and again, brought me back to putting things in priority, setting my mind straight when I had gotten caught in weird mind traps. She had taught me principles for getting along with myself and with others.

The greatest healing for me had come, however, when she had

opened her heart and let me see her own wounds. The best "medicine" she had given dripped from her own broken places as she let me in on her own heartbreaks, her failures, the areas that were "outcast" or unacceptable. Somehow, when she let me know that she, too, had suffered but had overcome, I was restored.

Indeed, God has brought others to be like the Good Samaritan to me, reaching out to what is outcast in me. Other faithful friends and strangers here and there have loved what I deemed unacceptable in myself. In a kind of hospitality of spirit, God's instruments have opened the doors of their own homes and their own lives and have embraced all of the parts of myself that I had tried to discard or hide. In the embracing, God's healing Spirit has poured through His instruments to help me become well.

Because of the constancy of my soul friendship with Sandra, however, I am keenly aware that there is never an encounter between us that is not undergirded with prayer. She prays about the details of my life between our meetings. She prays before I arrive. As we are visiting, she may become very quiet, or she might say, "Now let me see if I can hear what God has to say about that." Sometimes, in the middle of a conversation, she will stop and pray aloud.

Gradually, I got the point: God is the Divine Third Party between us and the power that emerges out of our encounters is directly related to the sensitivity of each of us to the promptings of God's Spirit. Sandra's example of humility, that willingness to listen to God's voice, showed me in a profound way the impact of the Good Samaritan. She incarnated—fleshed out—the love of Christ as she shared the strength that had grown from her own woundedness.

The thing about being an instrument of God is that He has to do some perfecting along the way. He takes any one of us just as we are, wherever we are, and He uses us as we are. However, because He has continually more challenging work for us, He has to do some tuning up here and there. Without that fine-tuning, I may rush out to do His work and mistake myself for a tool or a weapon, instead of His instrument!

I found that being an instrument of God puts me in His refiner's class. Attempting to obey God's direction in extending His grace creates some challenges. Again and again, the old must go in order to make room for the new wine if I am to be the most effective instrument.

I see now that God wanted to refine me so that I would be happier and more at peace with myself. He wanted to get me to the point of relying on Him for my own mental and emotional health. He wanted to draw me closer to Him so that I could come to know Him as the tender, loving Father/Friend He is.

It is clearer to me now than ever before that God transforms us so that we can be His hands and feet in the particular sphere where He has placed us. I see now that God has a great deal of work in breaking the shell of each ego in order to make soft hearts for His work. I didn't have a clue, when I started this venture, how much of my "ministry" was ego-based, but God has graciously let me know.

When I am under the influence of my ego, I use my insight, knowledge, and experience as weapons in the lives of others. Under my own power, I think that it is up to me to carve a little here, shave off some there, sand off the rough edges, and annihilate what is unacceptable in others. Telling others what they ought to be doing or lecturing them about what they should not be doing doesn't do much to heal the woundedness.

"Would you rather be right or happy?" someone asked, and I hate to confess that I had to give that question a good bit of thought. Much to my embarrassment, I discovered that my desire to be right was keeping me from being loving and forgiving and merciful and compassionate. That need to be right was keeping others at a distance and keeping me stuck in isolation. It was also rendering me ineffective to those who most needed a fresh word of grace. Being right extracts a great price and leaves me with very little.

I have learned the hard way that criticism never makes anyone change. Harping and nagging don't draw others into the Kingdom of God. A petulant, whiny spirit doesn't make anyone love me. Continually drawing attention to what is wrong doesn't seem to make things better, and withdrawing in a pout doesn't make anyone come running to see what they can do to make me feel better. Freezing others out never thaws cold hearts.

Living as a tool or a weapon makes walls between us, and it causes others' defenses to rise. When someone feels threatened in my presence, he will never let me be close to him. Presuming that I have the right to tell others what to do creates walls between us. My hardheadedness also makes my heart hard.

The reality is that people cause each other pain. Our selfishness and self-centeredness get in the way of our being instruments. We walk right over those we love in the name of the church, God, or good deeds, never pausing to sense their need, but forcing on them what we need to give.

We sit by each other in worship and never know the other's real feelings. We may rush out to collect food for people we hardly know while brushing by the emotionally needy all around us. The institutions that "should" help us often do not. Those we have counted on fail us. People let us down and we let others down. That is part of the human condition. We relive the actions of the Levite and the priest over and over.

Disappointment with others, however, can be used by God to bring about dependence on God. Coming to understand that every person has his line of limitation can be the beginning of a deepening friendship with the One who knows no limits. Giving up our dependence on human beings frees us to turn that dependence to the only appropriate Source, and then to live out of that security as an instrument of peace in the lives of others.

Living as an instrument of God (instead of living out of my own authority) changes the way I view every relationship. Taking seriously the mandate to "love one another" moves me from a position of taker to one of giver. Being willing to be the conduit through which God's presence flows makes my heart tender toward others.

The presence of Christ between us helps us to give up our myths about each other. Because He is the Spirit of Truth, His presence frees truth among us so that relationships can be built on the solid foundation of honesty instead of the shifting sands of deception.

The acceptance of Christ frees us to accept each other in our imperfections, and, somehow, that acceptance frees up energy that matures the relationship. Christ's presence frees the relationship to be what it was intended to be rather than conforming to my limited notions of what it should be. Christ's presence promotes tolerance.

When I take the presence of Christ into relationships, I am depending on Him to meet my needs instead of looking to others to meet those needs. My sense of His presence and authority acts as a protective checking when I might use another person as an object for my schemes. Knowing that Christ is all sufficient keeps me from being devastated when I remember that no human can ever meet all my needs.

"You don't own me just because you helped me!" was the shocking cry from someone for whom I was attempting to be God's instrument. I couldn't believe the ingratitude!

"You can't take over my life just because you helped me out in a hard time. This is none of your business!" a close relative informed me, and I picked up all of my best advice and went

86

home, sulking over the lack of appreciation for all I had done for her.

Early in my efforts to be God's instrument, I ran into the challenge of knowing and living the difference between "caregiving" and caretaking. Was I being helpful or harmful? People were telling me I was bossy or pushy. Then I began getting some clues that I was trying to take over others' decisions and responsibilities and, in doing that, I wasn't helping matters.

Caretaking is about abusing boundaries. A clear clue that I am caretaking is when I discover that helping you is hurting me. At other times, I finally figure out that I am caretaking when I become aware that I am angry with the person I'm trying to give care to, or when I am so burned-out with caring that I have nothing for the most significant others in my life.

Living out the call of Christ to be a servant opened up the startling discovery that I did not have the right to possess another person. I didn't have the right to determine how others would use their time or what they would do with their own giftedness. I came to understand that, just as Christ created and respected my individuality, I was called to accept and respect others' uniqueness and autonomy. As healing work was done in my own life, I became more and more able to love others without needing to own them or to cling to them. Finally, I was out from under the burden of thinking I had to provide the right answers, or, as a matter of fact, *any* answers!

It was quite a brutal awakening to discover that I was working harder on a friend's marriage than the partners were. I was expending a tremendous amount of energy helping facilitate communication between these two unwilling partners, winding up exhausted and resentful of their resistance to change. In taking on their responsibility, I was depriving them of the opportunity to solve their own problems.

"I'm working harder at this than you are," I finally blurted out.

"I think I care more about whether you stay together than you do." My friends agreed with me and proceeded to do what they wanted to do all along. They got a divorce and I learned an expensive lesson: Don't do for others what they should be doing for themselves.

"I'm afraid Sue will never get any better," I moaned to Martus one day after a group session in our living room.

"She may not," was his quiet reply.

I was stunned! What I really wanted was for Martus to assure me that the great advice and deep sensitivity I was giving this lady would pay off. I didn't want to be a failure—and my ego had convinced me that, if she didn't get any better, that would mean I had failed!

Another time, a handsome young man kept coming to me with the same problem over and over. I kept giving the same responses, attempting to be patient while he talked through the same issues *ad infinitum*. Later, I learned that his self-defeating behavior was escalating and that he was lying to me about his progress. Sadly, I had to acknowledge that he was using me to feed his narcissism and that I was of no help to him. This was one place God did not intend that I be an active instrument. (I do, however, continue to pray for him, recalling the months and years during which God has been patient with me.)

Continuing to bring relationships to God in prayer and continuing to visualize His presence between us is a terrific checks-and-balances system. Prayer frees me to offer what I know; but, more important, it frees me to offer myself to the other, to hear with my heart, to share my own journey, and then leave the other person free to make his own decisions.

I suppose the hardest place to be an effective instrument of God's grace is within the family system, but that is often where it is most needed. Without a sense of God's presence, family members tend to take on each other's responsibility or give each other blame. Because we are bonded to each other in such closeness, it is easy to believe that others cannot get along without us or that we must protect each other from the consequences of mistakes.

One of the most sensitive places is in the spiritual growth of family members. This should be treated with great caution. I am responsible to love my family, to nurture them, to encourage them, and to practice the presence of Christ in their midst. I am not responsible for playing God in their lives, and I am not the tour director for their spiritual journeys!

The truth is that caretaking is not true caring. Furthermore, it is a way of using others to meet my need to give care! If I am to give adequate and appropriate care, I cannot rely on my own wisdom alone. I need the constant support of Christ's presence to know the difference between the things I can change and the things I cannot. I need His convicting touch to stop when I tend to trespass in others' affairs. I need the strengthening presence of the Heavenly Father to give me what I need in order to let go of what is not mine. I must have habitual moments within the care of God to be able to give care fully and freely.

Staying connected in prayer is absolutely crucial when it comes to servanthood, for this is a primary area that is subject to misperceptions and errors. There is such a fine, invisible line between loyalty to God and loyalty to the other gods that pull the strings of my perceptions.

I would love to record that my efforts to be God's instrument have all been "successful," that everything I attempted worked just as I planned. The people I tried to help wanted to be helped. The projects I sponsored were filled with eager participants and always ran in the black. Everyone could see beyond my efforts to my pure motivations, and I didn't get any criticism along the way.

It would be so gratifying to report that I was able to stay out of my own way in my efforts to "be a blessing." I would love to report that my feelings have never been hurt and that I have always been able to stay cool under pressure in the processes of living out my call. I would also like to report that I have had unswerving powers of discernment and that wisdom flowed from my lips in ever-increasing fountains.

The truth is that living with the intent to be God's instrument creates all sorts of problems. Within my own nature, I discovered all sorts of invisible loyalties, ties to things and people I didn't recognize. In many ways, those unseen forces trapped me, strangling Christ's loving intent.

Somehow, attempting to maintain my primary loyalty—my loyalty to God—and to live under His direction, puts me in conflict with the voices of other loyalties in my head.

For example, I discovered that I have a loyalty to the "shoulds" and "oughts" that help me earn the approval of the particular society in which I live. I have a definition of how things should be and how I ought to behave. I have another agenda for how others should behave, and when they don't meet that agenda, I am upset.

Practicing the presence of God upsets those loyalties and expands my thinking to see as Christ sees. Prayer lifts the blinders from my eyes to see the ways my thinking is congealed, conformed to the world, and then it transforms my vision so that I can see through the eyes of Christ's love with clarity and peace.

It didn't take long for me to discover that I had a great tie to "what so-and-so would think" about what I was doing. Sometimes my perceptions of what others might be thinking or saying appeared as loud yakking on my part. But often it was a silent, inner disapproval dripping away at my self-confidence like a kind of spiritual water torture. That enmeshment with others' opinions ate away at my usefulness and efficiency. The energy and time I expended on others drained away my giftedness.

"Do what you need to do!" Martus has told me over and over through the years as I would fret about a particular decision. It took me years to realize that he was expressing confidence in my sensitivity to God's direction. Doing what I wanted to do seemed so selfish until someone explained to me that the very thing I wanted to do was usually God's call and that it was dangerous to walk away from that call. My invisible loyalties were distorting my primary loyalty.

I became aware, too, of the ways I let my loyalties to others keep me from being who God created and called me to be. Most of the time, however, that loyalty is to a certain role and the expectations I attach to that role.

I shudder to think how much time I have wasted not doing what I knew God had called me to do because I was trying to meet the agendas of others. In living by others' expectations, I did the tasks with resentment and never got around to doing what I knew I was supposed to be doing.

When I am true to my first loyalty, the responsibilities of other relationships also fall into line. Somehow, when I do what I am supposed to be doing after "seeking first the Kingdom of God," the parts of my life stay in balance.

Now and then in the evolution of language, a perfectly good word gets distorted and falls out of favor. I still remember my horror at using some word in an eighth-grade English class, only to have the students fall on their desks with glee. They had caught the teacher in her ignorance of schoolyard jargon.

For years, I have used the word *channel* (as in, "Make me a channel of blessing . . .") to describe the process of being filled with God's grace and then passing it on to the world. It was such a useful term, but I hesitate to use it now for fear of being mistaken as a psychic or spiritualist.

91

The word, however, adequately describes what happens as God mediates His love through human beings. The very picture of a channel brings up images of openness to receiving the flow of God's love. The picture isn't complete, either, without the image of that love flowing on out into the world. I don't want to give up my word; neither do I want to be mistaken in my use of it.

An outcast word reminds me of the people God places in my life as channels and instruments of healing. Often the healers seem to be the last ones I would have suspected. Sometimes the healing comes in ways I did not anticipate. At times I have said to myself, "Oh, no, not that one," both about people who have come to help me and about people I have been given to love. As always, God matches the giver and the receiver perfectly, though His ways may not be my ways.

There have been times when the greatest advice I have been given has been delivered in language that would make the Queen of England shudder. Some of the gentlest treatment I have received has been at the hands of rough people, smoothed by life's hardness. I have heard wisdom flow from the mouths of the young, and I have witnessed compassion in those whom society rejects. Sometimes God has used the outcasts of society to show me what is outcast in me, and thereby bring about deep, inner healing.

No matter how hard I work to hide what is wrong with me, God keeps on bringing that broken part of me out into the light of His love. He gently takes the outcast parts of myself and offers them as healing balm for others.

If I had known all that was to follow my prayer of commitment, I might not have had the courage to pray it. In the beginning, I had no way of knowing that no one can do for others what has not been done in us, and so the process of being Christ's instrument has to do with both giving and receiving. I cannot help others unless I have been helped, and in that necessary humility there comes the awareness that it's not *my* peace I am trying to establish. It isn't that I am trying to *keep* the peace, either, in a system of control and denial.

What I am called to do is be that channel of *His* peace within the world. He leads me to various people and places. He uses me to do His work in them, and He uses them to do His work in me. Each of us is called upon to be the wounded man and receive the oil of another's care; each of us is called upon to be the Good Samaritan. Prayer helps me to know which part of me God is calling out for His purposes.

I have discovered my woundedness in loving others. Loving others has caused woundedness, and yet it has become a way of knowing God. Knowing others in depth has become a way of knowing myself. In accepting the fact that I both need help and need to give it, I have, in a sense, come to "join the human race."

7
Look to the Other Side

We cannot love other human beings until we have some idea what human beings are like and how we can interact with them.

—Morton Kelsey

The Silver Rule: Do unto others as they want to be done unto.

—Hardy Clemons

. . . For the Lord does not see as man sees; for man looks at the outward appearance, but the Lord looks at the heart.

1 Samuel 16:7 NKJV

───◆───

Light and Dark.
Day and Night.
Hot and Cold.
Black/White. Yes/No. Up/Down. Independent/Dependent. Dry/Wet. Active/Passive. Theoretical/Practical. Masculine/Feminine. East/West. North/South. Soft/Hard. Opposites, all of them, made by God.

The more I practice relational praying, the more opportunities I have to learn new ways of relating to others. Committing my encounters to God, seeking His will in the midst of them, and acting as if He were physically present open all sorts of doors for change. It is like an ongoing on-the-job training program. I have noticed, too, that the education comes in unusual and interesting ways. The challenge is to be aware and awake enough to recognize God's activity.

My college-age daughter, Michelle, loves to bring home movies for us to watch together. The movies spark discussion between us and we both learn from the exchanges. One night, she brought home a movie that left us both speechless. It was as if the profundity of the movie stripped us of immediate responses.

The movie was a bizarre story about a culture of sameness. All the women of one class wore one type of garment, walked in rows at the same pace, and said the same stock phrases to each other. The efforts at sameness apparently were made to control the sin in that society. Fortunately, the human spirit transcended the efforts to erase uniqueness and individuality and to confine all people in the same cookie mold.

The movie stimulated my thinking about the fierce drive I have to uphold the differences in individuals. At the core of my being is the need to go beyond merely tolerating uniqueness to celebrating it. Even when others' freedom of expression goes against my grain or is at odds with my value system, I want others to have that freedom to be themselves.

There is something in me that rebels at the sameness of the stores that are emerging across our country. I resist doing things the way culture dictates just because everyone else is doing it. My belief in the right of the individual to be free comes from my theology. God made each of us as a unique and autonomous individual, accountable to Him, and He loved us enough to give each one the awesome, wonderful gift/burden of free will.

It is a never-ending source of interest to me that the church spread through the efforts of that ragtag band of Jesus' followers. Jesus chose a diverse group. He valued the impulsive Simon, whom He renamed Peter. Jesus needed James, who was a prac-

95

tical sort, as well as John, a contemplative, visionary guy. He needed the people-person strengths of Andrew, who was always going to get somebody else to join the band, and the independence and love for detail of the tax-gatherer, Matthew, whose very profession revealed his personality.

Using all different kinds of folks, Jesus formed a group that would carry the message. He knew that different strengths would be needed within the church, and that same mix of uniqueness is necessary today for vitality and creativity. We err when we attempt to stamp out that God-given diversity.

It intrigues me, as well, that the story of Jesus is told by four completely different personalities. Matthew valued details about Jesus' heritage, and he was interested in the teachings of Jesus. Mark's gospel is action oriented; his style is brief and to the point. Luke, the physician, wrote with the orderliness of a scientist and with a doctor's compassion. John looked beyond the details of events to their meaning. The style of each book is a reflection of the individual differences of each writer.

Later, Paul would flesh out the need for the diversity of gifts. In his letters to the various churches, he presented the image of the "body of Christ," with each valued part being used as it was designed to be used.

Each believer has a way to communicate the gospel in today's world. To be true to their temperaments, some folks must be aggressive and forthright in their presentation of the gospel, and there are those who respond to that method. I prefer a quieter, calmer, one-on-one approach, and God nearly always matches me with seekers who hear best on an individual basis.

Some respond to an orderly, rational, detailed study of the Bible, while others want a Bible study that emphasizes the relational aspect. The world is so needy that all the differing gifts and strengths are needed.

*   *   *

"I want to go on this mission trip," I told the coordinator of an area-wide partnership mission trip to Brazil, "but I don't want to hand out tracts on a street corner, and I don't want to go door-to-door conducting a survey."

After making such a strong pronouncement about what I didn't want to do, I felt guilty. After all, who was I to declare what I would and wouldn't do? I couldn't waste money just to "go along." What would I do when I got to Brazil? What would they let me do?

On our first night with Brazilian believers and American missionaries, I hesitantly approached one of the missionaries about the possibility of leading a small group for women. Much to my amazement, she seized my idea, got a translator, and organized our group. While others were doing what came naturally for them, I sat with twelve Brazilian women and, through a translator, conducted five sessions of a spiritual growth group.

I believe that those Brazilian women profited from the experience. I know that I will never forget the power that flowed among us as we shared our lives at a deep level. Throughout that week, as we explored concepts of God and how the presence of Christ changes relationships, it was obvious to me that the presence of Christ was there, teaching and instructing us, healing us and freeing us. God was in our midst, using us as instruments in one another's life, just as He was with the others who were going from door to door.

Perhaps my intense belief in individuality comes from years of feeling that I needed to be different from who I really was. I was naturally emotional, intuitive, and enthusiastic. But I bought into the culture's valuing of rational thinking and cool, reserved behavior. Only after many years of conforming did I develop the confidence to be the person God created me to be.

But perhaps God used those years of suppressing who I naturally was to create a drive in me to uphold others' freedom of expression, even when it goes against my grain. Perhaps my years of devaluing my innate strengths now serve as an impetus to bless others' differentness. Whatever the reason for my desire to affirm uniqueness, I will always believe that God worked in the midst of that process to bring me to wholeness and balance.

It was one of those watershed moments, a time fixed forever in my memory as a turning point. I even remember the way the room looked in the Pastoral Care and Counseling Center the night I was set free from a restricted way of thinking and seeing. I hadn't been on my spiritual growth journey for too many years, but I knew that this Bi/Polar Relationship Seminar had answers to questions I hadn't even verbalized.

"You know what would happen if you used only one leg," Hardy Clemons, our instructor, told us. Then he tried to walk with only one leg. "And you know that when a duck paddles with just one foot, he goes around in circles." We laughed at the absurdity of Hardy's proposition.

I could visualize everything Hardy was saying. In simple word pictures, he explained the significant Bi/Polar theory of opposites, especially those opposite, polar strengths in personality. I felt as though I was being led out of a dark tunnel into the light.

Hardy demonstrated the creativity that occurs by moving back and forth between thinking and doing. He went on to illustrate the necessity of both depending on self and depending on others, and he showed us the importance of developing both practical and theoretical thinking strengths.

Throughout the seminar, we were to discover ways each personality type gets stuck, or "polarized," when we overuse a strength until it becomes a weakness, and how it is possible to break that polarization and *change* to become a more productive and effective person. He showed us that it was even possible to develop those weaker areas, characteristics that lay dormant, un-recognized, and unused.

The more I listened to Hardy's explanations, the more it seemed that the whole room was filled with grace, and the grace was just for me. The more Hardy described my personality and temperament, the more lighthearted I became. It was not only okay for me to be "wired up" the way I was, but God Himself had made me that way! Now, all I had to do was learn to emphasize my natural strengths and build up my "lesser strengths," those attributes I thought I had missed when I was born.

I was so caught up in the blessing of discovering that my impulsive, sensitive, dramatic nature was okay that I hardly heard the rest of the seminar. It was overwhelming for me to realize that being intuitive was positive and that my energy and dynamism was part of what made me who I was.

For one who had spent her whole life trying to be practical and logical, it was truly good news to learn that theoretical thinking and the ability to be in touch with feelings were just as valuable as logic and reason. It was like being energized with some great fuel to discover that my dependent (or relational) personality was just as valuable as an independent one. Hearing my traits defined and discussed in a positive note was like hearing a new language. I couldn't believe the freedom I was experiencing.

Later, as Martus and I were trained to lead Bi/Polar Seminars, I came to a deeper appreciation of his traits, which I had always classified as "good," while giving mine a "bad" connotation. It was like being given a new lease on life. While he and I were indeed opposites, we could learn to work off each other's strengths and build up our own areas of lesser strengths. In other words, Martus had the capability of being a feeling person, and I could learn how to be logical and rational. There was hope!

Like most married couples, we had tried to work on each other through the years, criticizing the differences in temperament that had originally attracted us to each other. I was stuck in my theoretical thinking and my dependent relating; I had pushed my natural strength so far that it had become a weakness. I kept thinking that if I could just get Martus to be more sensitive and to express his feelings more, things would be better. He needed, I thought, to get out of his realism and dream a few dreams with me. If he could be more like I was, then we would have more in common and could get along so much better.

Martus, on the other hand, was polarized in his logical, practical thinking. He thought that if he could get me to be more practical, like he was, everything would be fine, but the more he tried to make me over in his image, the more stuck I became in my own polarization.

The more each of us tried to change the other, the more power struggles developed. In these times, criticism and judgmentalism prevailed where love and acceptance and delight in the other had once been the norm. However, with my new commitment to practicing the presence of Christ, I was increasingly uncomfortable with our attempts to remake each other. Somehow, trying to change Martus to fit my mold didn't fit with my new decision to be an "instrument of peace." Bi/Polar gave me a practical tool for acting on my praying.

Throughout my journey, God has consistently brought me the teacher that I needed when I was ready for the next lesson. For over ten years now, Martus and I have worked with the Bi/Polar system and have taught numerous seminars on the theory and practice of Bi/Polar. We continue to learn new things about differences in personality and the value of learning to flow back and forth between strengths. God continues to come to us through the process of reconciling seeming opposites.

Working with the Bi/Polar concepts through the years has been comparable to installing software in a computer. The Bi/Polar system has given me a framework for problem-solving in many areas. Bi/Polar has given me a practical pathway for creating balance in any area of my life.

Even in my prayer life, the Bi/Polar concept has been helpful in creating a satisfying and happy communion with God. I have learned that there are times when I need to "be still and know God" and there are times I need to get up and put my prayers into action. There are times when I need to pray in solitude, and there are times when I need to pray with some other human instrument. At times, I need to pray solely about personal concerns, and at other times I need to practice intercessory prayer. Sometimes I need the structure and stability of the same prayer pattern; now and then, I need to vary my routine so I won't become dull and flat.

A prayer life must be an active, vital part of life if it is to make a difference. There is a flow, a dynamism, to a fulfilling prayer life. To get stuck in one routine tends to create a numbing effect.

In leading prayer retreats and seminars, an understanding of differences in personality helps me to adapt different prayer experiences to different temperaments. Knowledge of the needs of personality types helps me make suggestions to others. Respect for individual differences keeps me from thinking there is only one "right" way to pray.

Practicing relational prayer keeps me open to learning from theological and cultural opposites, and it gives me enough humility to admit that there just might be truth in another point of view.

For over one-fourth of my life, and for more than half of our years of ministry, our denomination has been embroiled in a struggle of theology and power. My first reaction to the struggle? Try to ignore it. I have learned, however, that "denial is not a river in Egypt," but a deadly practice.

The truth is that the conflict has had some amazing benefits, for it has forced us who have grown up in the church to examine some of the basic beliefs and practices that we had taken for granted. In the polarization that has occurred—that is, the choosing of sides around extremes—we have learned some important things about ourselves and our beliefs. Without the conflict, we might have rocked along, numb in some very important areas.

In examining the extreme positions within our denomination, we have had to explore what we really believe. Coming to terms with the opposite of what we think, we have greater clarity about our own values and opinions. Confronting ways we do not want to live and worship, we have more clearly defined how we do want to live and worship. While it is true that much energy and time and money have been expended in dealing with the conflict, I believe that the conflict has not been wasted, for great creativity and productivity is released in the wrestling match between opposing polarities.

It was my privilege to travel through seven European countries with my sister, Bonnie, last summer. During that trip, I confronted cultural practices that were vastly different from my West Texas habits. Although there was some discomfort in feeling like an outsider, it was good for me to get out of my comfort zone and see different ways.

After attending the Passion Play in Oberammergau, Germany, Bonnie and I rode our assigned bus back to the tiny neighboring village of Ettal, located in a narrow mountain valley of the western Alpine foothills. Exhausted from our tour and from the lengthy play, we ate our dinner in the quaint hotel, and then Bonnie retired for the evening.

But there was something about the monastery across the street that called to me. So, in the last moments of daylight, I made my way across the narrow road and slipped into the monastery grounds through an ancient iron fence.

Sheep grazing on the mountain beyond the church greeted me. I could almost see Heidi bounding down into the village when I heard the bells on the sheep. Beautiful flowers lined the pathway to the church. I inhaled deeply, wanting to memorize each sight and sound and aroma to take home with me to the deserts of West Texas.

Slipping into the church, I caught my breath. The monks were inside, chanting their evening prayers! How could I have been so fortunate? I made my way to a seat and knelt, overwhelmed with the beauty of their singing, a singing that had filled that lovely Benedictine monastery since the 1300s.

Everything there stood in sharp contrast to the worship center of my home. Each act of worship was the opposite of what is done in my expression of the church. There, however, thousands of miles from home, in the gilded church of a secluded Catholic monastery, I worshiped the God-of-all-of-us.

The theory of opposites has touched and transformed my thinking about what it means to be a woman. I suppose the uproar around the issue of women's rights has created as much controversy as any of the cultural revolutions, and we in the church have been forced to rethink issues that have as much to do with sociology and culture as with theology.

During the past two years, one of the group processes within Growth Options, the organization I direct, has been a year-long exploration entitled "Healing the Masculine/Feminine Self." In that process, we have explored masculine and feminine strengths (again, another pair of opposites) in an attempt to bring balance to our own individual lives, and also to bring healing to male-female relationships. The process is fascinating, revealing, and sometimes painful.

We work with the concept that each of us is a combination of both feminine and masculine strengths. While our culture seems to value masculine strengths more, both are needed for creativity and fulfillment. True freedom comes in knowing when to em-

103

phasize each strength. Healing occurs as we recognize the areas that aren't quite "up to snuff."

Some of the feminine qualities are vulnerability, sensitivity, openness, cooperativeness, gentleness. Warmth, tenderness, receptivity, and patience are other qualities that might be called feminine, as well as softness, passivity, dependence, adaptivity, and nurturing. The feminine perspective tends toward being people oriented, flexible, and adaptive; the feminine aspects are seen in the ability to listen and wait.

Some of the masculine qualities are ambition, strength, independence, competitiveness, and confidence. We describe maleness in terms of being rational, dominant, virile, and powerful. Aggressiveness, rigidity, and a task-orientation also fit within the masculine structure. The masculine aspect is one of proclaiming, declaring, telling, and pronouncing.

As in the Bi/Polar system, trouble comes when one side of the polarity is emphasized to the exclusion of the other. When the masculine strengths get overemphasized in an individual or in a culture, there is too much aggression and competitiveness, and there is a tendency toward legalism.

When there is too much of an emphasis on the feminine strengths, there is a soppiness and sentimentality. Too much adapting leads to co-dependency and unhealthy loyalties. Too much nurturing leads to weaknesses in those being overnurtured.

It seems obvious to me that real liberation needs to come for both men and women. Both sexes need to embrace both polarities of masculinity and femininity, not to create a unisex, but to expand the possibilities of relating. Men need to access their vulnerability and be free to express their gentleness just as women must know when to be assertive and direct.

Again, prayer leads to awareness of what is broken—both within my personality and between myself and others. As we continue to bring that brokenness to Christ's healing presence, we find harmony and peace. Practicing the presence of Christ within relationships opens our eyes to see clearly what is out of balance.

There are ramifications of the concept of the masculine/ feminine balance even in the actual meditation experience. In my praying, there are times when I need to call on the gentle, tender, nurturing side of God. In those times, I meditate on the words in Psalm 131:2: "I have stilled and quieted my soul; like a weaned child with its mother, like a weaned child is my soul within me."

In picturing the tender side of God, I love to "call up" those scenes from the gospels when Jesus portrayed the Father's gentle, tender Spirit. I visualize Him with the children; I put myself into the scenes of healing as if I were the one receiving His nurturing touch. I mull over the vulnerability of Christ as He lived out His life and His death with such openness.

At other times, I need to meditate on the power and strength and might of God the Father. In practicing the presence of Christ, I need to recall those attributes of God that are about action and assertiveness. The key for me is to remain open (a feminine strength) to the Spirit of God. He will give to me the image of Himself that I need for that moment.

As I surrender to the process of inner praying, God's Spirit also does the work that needs to be done in bringing balance to my own personality. One of the ways He works is in using others to get my attention about what is out of balance.

"I wish I weren't so sensitive," I wept, complaining about the burden of feeling so deeply about a situation.

"You need to know when to let things fly over your head," counseled a friend who doesn't notice slights or insults. I knew that what she was saying was true, and yet the more I tried to let things roll off, the more they seemed to stick to me.

Prayer has a most practical side to it, for through praying I come to discernment about when I am allowing my feminine side to get stuck. I am also brought to conviction when I am polarized in my aggressive, masculine side and tend to run over people or get too bossy with my directives. As I consult the Director of my life, He quickens my sensitivity to what is out of balance and then provides the strength to move out of my rut and into balance.

The Bi/Polar Seminar offers a simple formula for dealing with the opposites in our personalities and in our relationships. The system calls for respect, assertiveness, and equality.

Frankly, I need the constant prompting of God's Spirit in dealing with the delicate dances of intimacy. Left to my own natural way of relating, I tend to create disharmony or distance. With the conscious effort to maintain contact with God, I find the freedom and the strength to know how to act in balance. Sharing the splendor of Christ's freeing love goes better when I keep the following qualities of the Bi/Polar system in mind.

Respect

Respect within a relationship means that I value your temperament and take into account your individuality when I approach you. It means that I listen to what you are saying rather than laying my words or interpretations on your words. Respect requires me to allow you to think your thoughts and to hold your own opinions. It means that I don't attempt to play God in your life, but allow God to deal with you as He will.

Respect means that I do not violate your space, your person, or your freedom of choice and that I am conscious of the impact I am making on you. Respect cannot exist where there is physical, spiritual, sexual, verbal, or emotional abuse or neglect, for those qualities are mutually exclusive.

Respect means that I honor the reality that you are made in

the very image of God. It also means that I acknowledge that God just might be speaking through you to me. It means that I don't try to convict you of your sins, but allow God to have that right.

"You are overwhelming me with your barrage of words," Martus told me through shaving cream one morning as we got ready for the day. "Just tell me what you think without coming on so strong. I need some respect."

I was insulted. *If only he would give me a response,* I thought, *then I wouldn't have to repeat my opinions so often and so vehemently!*

I stood there, watching him shave, and realized that a beginning point in giving respect would be to approach him sometime when he wasn't cornered, either by time or space. After all, it was pretty disrespectful to hit somebody with big decisions that early in the morning.

"How can I communicate respect to you and still get my point across?" I inquired, never thinking for a moment that he could come up with an answer in the limited time I had. I like quick responses; Martus gives studied, careful ones.

"Speak more softly, and just ask me one time," he replied. "I can hear you better if you won't be so aggressive or so loud."

I still hadn't gotten an answer to my original dilemma, but I had to concede that he had a point. If I was going to get a response from him, I was going to be forced to learn a more respectful way.

I slipped behind the door, closed it nearly all the way, and through the crack in the door, whispered, "Martus, I need to talk with you. . . ." We both burst into laughter at my ridiculous approach. Humor saved the moment. I learned a lesson about respect, and he gave me the answer I needed to a pressing question.

Assertiveness

A relationship needs respect, but it also calls for a quality that brings action and dynamism to it. Every relationship, if it is to be what God intended it to be, requires *assertiveness*. Each partner in the relationship needs to invest in the relationship. Each person's energy is needed. Each person needs to take responsibility for making things happen within the relationship; a one-sided relationship leads to control or passivity.

Assertiveness takes the form of appropriate speaking up within the relationship, and that appropriateness must be carved out within every relationship to fit the partners involved. Assertiveness involves taking charge and initiating, doing things for the other person and for the friendship. Assertiveness both reveals and fosters ownership of the relationship; it is a rule of life that we value those things in which we have put time, energy, money, and emotion.

"You care too much about what we do," each of my girls has, at one time or another, protested about my concern with where they go and what they do. Sometimes their protests have been valid, but, more often than not, they have simply been squirming under parental questioning. (That is my perspective, not theirs, but since I have the word processor, I get to give my point of view!)

"Of course I care, and I care passionately about what you do," I am quick to tell these teenagers who are so eager for independence. "You are the most important people in my life and I have invested years of care and nurturing and love in each of you. I'll never stop being interested in your lives!"

At this point, the girls roll their eyes and continue to protest that I am smothering them. I think they know, however, that they are cared for and that I am attempting to give them the amount of freedom that fits their development and maturity.

Assertiveness means, too, that I tell the truth within the relationship and that I don't hide behind defenses. Here also the Spirit of Truth is the teacher and guide, helping me to see with clarity what needs to be said and done, and then giving me the courage to do what is best for the relationship.

Equality

Equality is the third ingredient necessary for balancing the delicacies of relationships.

"I don't mind your having an equal vote," a friend of mine told his wife, "but I want my vote, too!" What a challenge it is to carve out equality among strong-willed, independent, self-seeking human beings. For those who find it hard to give others as much value as themselves, it is hard, and for those of us who think others are worth more, it is hard. Equality is a delicate dance of balance.

Meeting others straight-across, as equals in God's eyes, regardless of who they are, what position they hold, or how old they are, requires a degree of humility. Avoiding the one-upmanship trap, where one is down and another is up, we can express the freeing love of Christ, who related to all in a perfect balance of respect and assertiveness. Jesus Christ knew when to act and when to wait. As we depend on His promptings, we can learn how to treat others with equality.

With the practice of relational prayer, the spirit of equality prevails naturally. After visualizing Christ sitting down with me and another person, I cannot keep that person above me or below me. In Christ's presence, social or religious hierarchies disappear and the lines of class or age fade. With Christ as the Divine Third between us, status and power don't seem to matter. It is difficult to hold an "I'm right, you're wrong" point of view in the presence of the Prince of Peace.

Christ is the equalizing partner in a relationship. Listening to His promptings with a soft heart and an open mind keeps me from erecting artificial walls and distinctions and helps me see both parties—myself as well as the other—as His child, loved and cherished by Him.

The opposites of life can torment us. Those same opposites can be instruments of healing and wholeness and joy. Surrendered to the power of God and seen as an opportunity for growth and balance, the opposites offer infinite possibilities.

8
Power Transformed

Control is an illusion. It doesn't work. I can't change other people.

—Melody Beattie

Each of you should look not only to your own interests, but also to the interests of others. Your attitude should be the same as that of Christ Jesus.

Philippians 2:4, 5

———— ❧ ————

"Forgive us our trespasses, as we forgive those who trespass against us."

Often, when I am walking, I pray the Lord's Prayer several different times, pausing to mull over the phrases or words that seem to want my attention. While I don't believe there is anything magical about repeating the words, or praying the prayer a designated number of times, I have discovered great power in saying the prayer several times as a form of meditating, allowing the ancient, beloved words to center me in the awareness that I am a child of the Heavenly Father.

On one warm summer morning, my attention kept coming back to the part about forgiveness of trespasses. This time, however, my focus was on the *trespassing* issue rather than the forgiveness. Again, as I have learned to do, I recognized that mental turning as a nudging of God's Spirit. I didn't worry or fret about what the meaning was for me, but simply allowed the words to be in my mind. I knew that God would reveal the truth He wanted me to have, and so I simply rested in the process.

The words haunted me throughout the day. I wondered why some of us use *debts* in that phrase, while others say *trespasses*. I could easily understand the importance of the forgiveness of debts, but I didn't have a clear picture of this trespassing problem. All that would come to my mind was a "No Trespassing" sign on a vacant lot.

Later that evening, when my mind had rested and I wasn't straining to come up with some great pearl, the truth came to me. There, right in the middle of the Lord's Prayer, was an outright acknowledgment of a major problem among people. Jesus Himself knew that we would trespass in others' affairs and that we would allow others to trespass in ours. He knew that intimacy would evoke a problem in balancing freedom, power, and belonging.

The meaning of my meditation time suddenly revealed itself. As much as I didn't want to admit it, God was bringing my problem with *control* to my attention. As I attempted to bring my thoughts and my ways under the control of Christ's teachings, I was going to be compelled to look at the power struggles in my life.

Control is the way of relationships that are based on fear. It takes as many forms as there are individuals. Some control overtly, bossing and bullying others, while others are silent controllers, using looks or behavior to get others to do what they want them to do. I recognized that I had a vast repertoire of ways of controlling *and of being controlled by others*. God had a lot of work to do with me!

People control others instead of loving them in order to gain power over them. Some people control because they can't trust others. They feel the whole deal rests on their shoulders. How many of us controlling types have nearly killed ourselves with that powerful little hook, "If it is to be, it's up to me."

Some control because they are desperate for love and will do whatever it takes to elicit the response they want. Some attempt to plot and scheme in order to gain self-esteem and to prove to themselves that they are worthy. Control is an especially sinister problem within religious circles for those of us who feel we must "save" others, forgetting that God Himself allows us to choose hell, if we must.

Some of us stay in control because we want to keep up appearances, keep others' actions hidden from view, or because we are afraid of our own emotions. We control to put off the inevitable or to keep from having to face the truth.

"Control really isn't my problem," a group member said last week, but this was after a lengthy description of the phone calls she had made to tell her version of a family affair. "If I can just keep everyone from getting mad at each other, we'll all be okay." How easy it is to see control games in others, and how hard it is to recognize our own.

Surrendering my will to a friendship with Christ necessitates a change in the way I love. Conforming to the image of Christ calls for a complete renovation. No longer can I get by with doing things according to the world's standards; I must always be conscious of my tendency to abuse power.

If you take a tour through any bookstore today, you will discover a plethora of books addressing the problem of women who love too much and men who can't commit to an ongoing relationship. There is much written today on people of both sexes who go too far in loving, and those who don't quite go far enough. Books abound on the problem of control and manipulation between individuals. Apparently, the reading public is now aware that there is more to getting along with each other than simply doing what comes naturally, for what comes naturally is often

113

dysfunctional, immature, counter-productive, or unsatisfying. Inquiring minds want to know what it takes to love someone without losing one's own self.

The first few times I heard a facilitator in a small group talking about "owning one's personal power," I didn't have a clue as to what she meant. My mind didn't have the software to hold such a topic. My instructor might as well have been speaking Chinese when she urged us to take responsibility for the power we had.

Through the next few years, however, life would install the software in my mental and emotional computer. I would come to understand, by living and loving, that it is possible to love you without giving up me. I would, by identifying my own control issues and my fears, begin to reconcile the tension created between my often conflicting needs for both independence and dependence.

Telling me that I had *power* was like giving a Mercedes to a monkey. I went from not being aware that I had any power to using it in all the wrong ways. I was indeed a beginner in this venture, a child who was learning to walk, and in the process, I stumbled and fell a lot.

With long years of trying to avoid responsibility for myself, I had avoided the use of power by withholding. I expected others to know what I wanted. If they loved me, they could guess what I needed. When I did try to take charge, it was often too late or too little—or, on the other extreme, too much and too often.

"Whoosh!" my second daughter, Julie, says to me when I come on too strong with an edict. To add to her dramatic flair, she pulls her hair back, as if a great wind has just blown her hair back.

At first I couldn't figure out why she was reacting to my suggestions and requests. Finally it dawned on me that what seemed like a simple request on my part was perceived by my family as a tornado. *To make up for my feelings of helplessness and to over-*

come my fear of being assertive, I would deliver a simple request with the force of a cannon shot.

Neither did I know that my avoiding the rightful use of power within a relationship was itself causing me to drift into *control*. I tried to control others' responses to me and to each other. I tried to control what my children thought, who their friends were, and what they did, but in sneaky, covert ways so they wouldn't catch on to my game.

I didn't realize that it was not up to me to make anyone happy or successful, and so I tried controlling their feelings about themselves and others. Now I know that the less control I feel over my own self, the more I try to exert over others.

The interesting thing about control is I may not see it in myself, but I can certainly identify another's control! In the beginning, none of my controlling is ever conscious. My technique seems so natural and my motivation so pure to me that I can dupe myself into believing that I am just doing the right thing. It is other people who manipulate!

Control of others is a learned response, a habit that can be changed. Controlling of others is about violating another's personhood. Control is trespassing into what really isn't my business, and it usually emerges in people who have had others trespass in their lives.

Once the Spirit of Truth convinces me that I do have a problem with control, I bring the problem to my prayer time. I visualize Christ sitting between me and the person I am in conflict with or want to understand better. I ask for the ability to see the areas where I am exerting control, and *every single time* I see.

The presence of Christ opens my eyes and reveals the subtle, manipulative ways I try to motivate others. His presence also makes me see that control is a way of lying, for it is trying to get others to do what I want them to do in an underhanded, deceptive way.

In my meditation time, I am more and more convicted about this control issue. In the beginning, I was ashamed of the ways I had hidden my agendas from others, and I was astounded at how others often knew that I was trying to pull their strings or punch their buttons. My prayer time opened up all sorts of unpleasantness for me, but I knew that if I was ever to have true *empowerment*, I had to walk through this valley.

In His graciousness, God showed me that my control games create resistance in others—even when they aren't aware of my control game. I didn't recognize this, however, until I got in touch with my own feelings about people who attempt to control, "parent," or gain power over me. By becoming aware of my own reactions, I learned that my children's agitation with me is often directly related to my trying to live their lives and make their decisions. Confrontations that "blindside" me frequently start in some hook that I "innocently" put out. In prayer, I had to confess that I do my part to light the fires of conflict.

When there is a relationship that is out of sorts now, I can count on getting acquainted with one of my control issues. Thankfully, though, I can also rely on God's patience and participation in the correcting of the problem. He never brings a problem to my attention without also providing a way out of the problem. The Deliverer works full-time.

Giving up control of another human being can be the pathway out of my own bondage. Laying down the power struggles creates opportunities for empowerment by the loving Spirit of God. Putting things in their rightful perspective, letting God be God, and minding my business, leads to harmony and peace.

The process of finding balance between my needs and your needs is best facilitated when I intentionally bring the presence of Christ into the dynamics, acknowledging Him as the only source of real power, and surrendering my power to His within the relationship. I stay on course best when I maintain relational prayer.

If power struggles are part of the human condition, how do we live with them? How do we maintain conscious contact with God when all of these earthly beings are in our faces, complicating our schedules and our balance sheets? How do we live out Christ's commandment to love God and our neighbor as ourselves? How do I take care of my needs and your needs without resorting to power plays and manipulative ploys? Where do I find the grace to be honest in love?

How is it possible to walk that balance beam between individuality and belonging without falling off on either side? How do I reconcile my need for closeness and my need for autonomy? What do I do when my selfishness rears its head? How do I become more of an individual when my pattern is to give too much of myself away?

I can read all of the relationship books on the shelf, and I can attend seminars and classes on learning how to communicate. I can do any number of things to improve the dynamics between myself and others. By my own skill and cunning, I can make significant changes in the way I get along with others.

The most powerful key of all, however, is in the first part of Christ's command: Love the Lord your God with all your heart, mind, and soul. Christ put first things first. He gave the vertical relationship, His communion with His Heavenly Father, first priority. He sought first the Kingdom; that is, He took care of His first task—lining Himself up with the Father's will—and then everything else fell into its proper place.

Loving God first keeps me from putting another person up or down in a power struggle. Prayer brings my will into conformity with God's will so that I will not impose my will on others. Meditation keeps me seeing the ideal, and yet tolerating the actual. Relational prayer takes the energy wasted in the power struggles and transforms that energy into a healing force.

I have not yet found a better way to correct misdirected and misused power than to keep on coming to my quiet time with all the concerns of my life. The Scriptures will, if I allow them to, always give me the principles I need. Friendship with Christ always guides me in the transformation of my human friendships.

"Okay, I know this is a power struggle, but how do I stop it?" boomed the big voice of a man in trouble with his wife. "I can see the problem, but you've got to tell me what to do about it."

Sam, a big and burly man, had a history of control and power problems. The mere fact that he was sitting in my office was painful evidence that he was hurting, and hurting badly. To put himself in a position of admitting a problem and asking for help went against the grain of everything he had been taught about what real men did.

Sam grew up in a culture that perpetuated the unwritten rule that a man's vote counts more. His time is more important than his wife's, and his job is more valuable than hers. His opinions carry more weight, and his needs take precedence over anyone else's needs.

Until this point in his life, Sam had not only gotten away with being bigger and better and brawnier than everyone else, he had succeeded in his power plays. In the eyes of the world, Sam was a success, able to wield power with the best of them.

The only problem was that, at home, those closest to him had decided that *their* votes counted as well. They were tired of the constant stream of advice. What Sam's family wanted was not so much his telling them what to do as his being with them. Sam's friends, as well, wanted to be friends without feeling that they had to defer to his agenda and his moods.

Sam was in big trouble. Furthermore, he had begun a spiritual quest, and that deep, inner voice was letting him know that something needed to be brought into conformity with the image of Christ.

"A place to begin is in detaching," I suggested. "What would happen if you slowed down before you reacted to your daughter's rebellion? How would it be different if you could withdraw from the problem enough to observe what you are doing that causes a reaction from others?"

Sam knew enough about the dynamics of power to know exactly what I was talking about, but he wasn't sure he could carry it off. "I have used power for so long," he said, "that I would feel defenseless without it."

Without intending to, Sam spoke a great truth about power. When we feel afraid, we come on too strong. Fear and insecurity cause us to try to play a game of one-upmanship. However, control can't hide forever your fear of being known as you really are. Eventually, life calls its hand.

Detachment provides a safe way to stay involved in a relationship without being enmeshed in it. Detachment seems to be part of the secret of the effectiveness of Christ. He was able to do what needed to be done when it needed to be done because He got His identity from His relationship with His Heavenly Father. Christ didn't need to exert earthly power because He was empowered with divine love.

Detachment is a process of disentangling myself from the emotions of the moment and becoming aware of what is going on. It means allowing others to be who they are. Detaching means that I *listen* to what is going on inside my head and that I listen to what others are saying. Detaching requires me to take my responsibility, of course, but *only* my responsibility, and not yours.

Those who have been involved with chemical-addicted loved ones know the necessity of tough love. They know that sometimes the only chance you have at salvaging a relationship is by laying it down, giving it up, and turning it over to the hands of God. While the concept of detachment has been widely promoted in the recovery programs of various kinds, detaching works in all transactions.

"I tried detaching from my friend last week," Sally told us in a spiritual growth group, "but it felt as if I were cold and uncaring."

For those of us who have misused power and fallen into control, detachment does feel unnatural. There have been more times than I can ever remember when I have prayed for God to fill me with the courage to detach and then help me through those agonizing moments of letting go.

"Let's go out to eat," I said to Martus one evening. I had been working all day and had not had time to prepare a meal. The children were all occupied in evening extracurricular activities, and it seemed a perfect opportunity to spend an evening together away from the responsibilities of the home front.

"Okay, we'll go out to eat," Martus responded. He said the right words, but my heart fell. The words didn't match the tone of his voice. Which message should I believe, the verbal or the nonverbal one? Should I ignore his obvious resistance and go on with my plans, or should I respond to his body language, which shouted no, and come up with something from the pantry?

Through the years of teaching Couples' Communication, Martus and I have become acutely aware of the power that language has in shaping the dynamics of relating. Mixed messages, when the words say one thing and the body language, facial expression, and tone of voice say the opposite, create chaos.

Such fuzzy and unclear communication can be a power game. So can the withholding of one's real opinions, needs, feelings, and thoughts. These can be dishonest ways of maintaining control of the other person or the relationship. Shooting straight is a great way to keep relationships clear of the debris of control.

In teaching communication styles, I have become increasingly aware of the significance of Jesus' teachings on "letting your yes be yes, and your no be no." Jesus' style of communication was one of "say what you mean, and mean what you say," and there is no better foundational principle for creating freedom and grace among us than that. Good, clean, and clear communication is a deterrent for power struggles.

Jesus was a master communicator, spending a great deal of time in dialogue with His disciples. He said exactly what needed to be said to the person before Him. He was clear and direct, honest and forthright. Jesus made Himself vulnerable with His communication, speaking directly from His heart so that those who had ears could hear.

Jesus not only listened to the words the person was saying, but He was also able to sense the meaning behind the questions and the comments of others. He met each person at the point of his need.

Part of the process of being transformed into His likeness is taking responsibility for the power of communication, the art of sending and receiving information. Part of what separates us from animals is our God-given ability to reason with each other. Because I believe so strongly that communication is a primary key in creating love and in living the Kingdom life, I take seriously the need to develop skills in communication.

There is infinite healing power in talking together, in revealing awareness to each other. Sharing my awareness with others with both discernment and courage is a way of sharing myself. Hearing another person's truth about what he feels, thinks, wants, and senses is a way of sharing life at its deepest level. Doing away with as many secrets as possible is one way of unclogging the power lines and moving out of the darkness into the light.

121

"Why can't I talk with my family the way I talk with this group?" individuals often ask in spiritual growth groups. The willingness to be transparent in the group often stands in stark contrast with the strangled communication at home.

Of course, it is easier to be transparent with people who aren't quite so close and with whom there is not so much at stake. However, group members discover that practicing the skills of transparency in a small, safe group increases their courage to be transparent in more intimate and, potentially, more sensitive relationships.

I always feel loved when I have been with someone who is willing to entrust himself with me. When others share their lives through words, I feel I'm a part of them, and they, a part of me. Communication helps me know that I am not alone; it keeps me remembering that I am a part of the family of God.

While it is true that some of us are born with more verbal abilities than others, it does not necessarily mean that we are more able to talk intimately with each other. In fact, it is often those of us who talk the most who are trying to hide behind our words. Real communication doesn't come naturally. Like community, communication is something that must be learned and practiced, but it is a powerful tool for getting acquainted, solving problems, resolving conflicts, and building true intimacy.

There is a spiritual principle that can be applied to the art of communicating. Whenever I use whatever talent I have in hearing and speaking, it expands. Whenever I bury my abilities, refusing to use them, I lose what I have.

Talking together is a way of releasing healing, grace-giving love. For partners who are willing to be aware that Christ is present, it is a way of practicing relational prayer with eyes open or shut.

"It's quality time that counts" was the myth of the seventies and eighties, a terrible lie that we told each other to justify all our rushing around. The lie kept us from facing the truth that we were neglecting each other.

You can't have quality time together unless there is quantity. Intimacy doesn't happen suddenly or on the run, and rushing around is a way to avoid the pain and problem of getting close. Staying too busy is one of the ways we try to make ourselves think we are in control. Driven to be powerful in the eyes of the world, we create distance and disharmony.

"Just be here with me," is a request I'll never forget. "I don't want you to do anything for me. I don't even want you to talk to me, necessarily. Just stay here awhile."

With that request, I came face-to-face with my fear of closeness. Didn't I need to fill up the silence with noise or action? Shouldn't I be doing something? Simply being still made me feel out of control and edgy.

I have learned, when that fear of losing control rears up, to breathe deeply and give up the fear. I visualize myself resting back in the chair and then I do that. I rest my hands, palms up, in my lap to remind myself that I am open to the promptings of Christ. I turn my inner ear to pay attention to any guidance from the One who created us for relationships, and then I look into the eyes of the person God has given me for that moment.

The greatest gift Christ has given is His presence, and the greatest gift we can give each other is presence. Being together, without an overriding, driving agenda, is a way to access love's healing force. Being together, without the need to control or be controlled, is a pathway of peace.

Some of the deepest communion I have had with others has come in those moments when we have taken time to walk together along a mountain path or a city street, with no pressure to fill up the silence with chatter. Some of the greatest peace and understanding I have known with loved ones has been in the car, on long stretches of highway, when no one felt forced to "share," but each chose to talk about what was going on in his own individual journey. I know about the quality of love that is set loose on a winter's evening before the fireplace or on a summer afternoon beside a mountain stream, when there is no hurry to get anywhere else.

As we take time to be together, we can give up the games of control. When we slow down, we can see how the power struggles are eating away at our mutual love and respect. Together, we can see it is safe to share ourselves honestly.

It is no accident that the Lord's Prayer has a twofold plea for forgiveness. Jesus knew that each of us would need to ask both to be forgiven and for the power to forgive. He knew how common it would be for us to sin against one another.

One of the reasons I must practice regular meditation and stay involved in accountability processes with people who are serious about the spiritual journey is that I need to keep my forgiveness accounts current. Both of those activities—praying and being accountable—are essential in helping me forgive and receive forgiveness myself.

Last year, I became aware that I was holding on to a particularly difficult problem. I kept beating myself and others for this problem, and the more I prayed about it, the more the issue dogged me.

I didn't really want to talk with my spiritual director about this problem. I used all sorts of excuses to convince myself that it was too petty for her to deal with. I tried to dupe myself into thinking it really wasn't all that bad. The bigger problem was that the more I avoided dealing with the truth, the more I had to work to stay in control in my relationships. I couldn't believe there was such a profound connection between telling the truth (confession) and my control problem.

I have discovered that one of the most devious tricks of the Evil One is to mess with my memory. Too easily, I forget how my self-defeating actions *always* make results I don't want, and I can't seem to remember how powerful confession is. I forget (or stuff) the memories of those who hurt me, and I conveniently forget (or deny) the hurtful things I do to others.

If I stay in regular communion with Christ, however, He works on my memory, and I am compelled to follow the pathway of freedom. Finally, I made my confession. As always, that confession released a power that I am learning to remember. The truth set free within my own heart releases truth between myself and the significant others in my life.

According to the scriptural pattern, we should use things and love people. Yet, with all our power struggles, we humans tend to turn that principle upside down. In our distorted views about God, man, and the universe, it is far too easy to use people and love things.

My tendency to use people emerges when I cling too tightly to people. Out of fear, I try to possess my friends, clinging to them and expecting them to do what I want them to do because I want them to do it.

My spiritual journey made me face the truth about how I used others as a security blanket, clinging to them out of loneliness and need. As I began to get more and more of my identity from my relationship with Christ, I saw that I was holding on to others and keeping them from their own relationship with Christ. I used all sorts of rationales to maintain my clinging: I needed to protect or help or "guide" others.

The irony, I discovered one day in my prayer time as I was writing a stream-of-consciousness exercise in my journal, was that one of my pet peeves was others' clinging to me. "If there is anything I can't stand," I complained, "it is for someone to think she owns me. I can't tolerate possessive people!" Again, my gift of projection was in full swing, as I attempted to stay in the driver's seat at all times.

Jesus' pattern for loving was setting people free. He allowed others to be who they were. He respected individuality and never forced Himself or His will on anyone.

In that poignant, heartrending moment in the Upper Room, Jesus held out the morsel of friendship—and, I think, of escape—to Judas. Even at the last moment, Jesus held on to the hope that Judas would relent and enter into the love relationship Jesus intended. However, when Judas chose to go and follow his own willful plan, Jesus let him go.

Intimacy and closeness are beautiful realities. Just as important and just as sacred as those moments of communion, however, are the spaces between us. The ability to draw apart, the willingness to allow separateness—these are part of love's challenge and love's gift. To live at peace with the awareness that others are free to go their own way, and not be threatened by that, helps to empower the relationship.

Fortunately, the Spirit of God keeps me moving out of the cocoon of perceived safety I have woven for myself and into the freedom of loving. He allows others and me to follow the pathway of wholeness. I would like to say that that journey is completed and I am no longer a controlling person. It would be such an ego trip to be able to declare that I am thoroughly enlightened and that I now use power wisely and well.

The truth is that I get one day's reprieve. Each day, I must begin again with a beginner's mind. Each day, I recognize that unless I surrender myself to the power of God, I will misuse power over others, and I will try to control with a myriad of games and rackets. To the extent that I surrender my will to God's, He keeps me knowing where the real power lies. He, with His tender love, empowers me to live and love with His kind of love.

For me, a recovering sinner, that is Good News.

9
Staying In

For marriage, as simply as it can be defined, is the contemplation of the love of God in and through the form of another human being.

—Mike Mason

. . . What God has joined together, let man not separate.

Matthew 19:6

———◦◦◦◦———

"You might as well give up expecting me to love you like your mother did."

Bob was an enlightened husband. With that straightforward suggestion to Barbara, his wife, he identified a core problem of the marriage and opened up several areas of growth for the relationship. Both Bob and Barbara had placed spiritual growth at the top of their priority lists for many years. Now, within their marriage, they were reaping the rewards of their faithfulness.

Bob knew that those unrealistic expectations were blocking the energy in their marriage and keeping his wife from accepting the love and faithfulness he lavished on her. He also knew that those expectations were blinding her from seeing the worth and health that was in the marriage. She was so committed to accepting only her view of the marriage that she couldn't allow the marriage to be what it was.

When Bob made his declaration to Barbara, he also exposed

the tendency of individuals to look for someone, somewhere, who will finally be all things to them. How common it is to expect one's marriage partner to be the Perfect Parent. Often, that pressure destroys what is basically a good marriage.

"None of the women I date loves me," is a cry heard from the unenlightened, but the cry is all too common. While most of us choose a partner in some mysterious selection process, we usually choose someone we think will love us. When the honeymoon is over and the gift of disillusionment comes, then comes the best part: deciding to love the other. Maturing to the point of giving instead of demanding within marriage is the point at which true, spiritually vibrant marriage is possible.

Not only does human marriage bear the Perfect Parent expectation, but some expect it to take the place only God can take. In our desire for unconditional love, we expect human marriage to be what only the divine romance can be. In our confusion, we demand unconditional love from broken, imperfect, needy humans, while refusing to go to the only Source of perfect love.

The participants in a pre-Easter Quiet Day fanned out across the wide lawns of the Christ the King Retreat Center. I had given them a procedure that would require at least a couple of hours of solitude. Sensing that these retreatants could make their own way through the silence, I slipped down to the edge of the river, where I could be available, if needed, but out of the stream of activity.

Spring in West Texas, like the spiritual journey and like marriage, can be violent, but more often there is a beauty and gentleness to it. This was one of those perfect days, a day with a brilliant blue sky and just the right temperature.

Perched on the riverbank, and shaded by the new leaves of tall pecan and oak trees, I watched the river's lazy motion. The Concho is a gentle river that cuts a tender route across San

Angelo, and on this day its quiet ripplings provided the perfect external picture of my mental wanderings.

Now and then, a water creature would bubble up to the surface, and I would watch the effects rippling across the surface. Periodically, a bird would fly into my vision, pause for a moment, and then be on its way to another destination. Nature created a sanctuary for me, a place and a mood for a significant encounter. My Quiet Day focus, which I hadn't consciously planned, would be a turning point.

When I first began making silent retreats, I would carry an agenda with me. I would use that time to pray about a specific issue or problem, hoping to get some direction or guidance. I didn't realize that by focusing on that one issue, I was often either praying to the problem and increasing my agitation, or I would miss the gift that God had for me for that time. It took me years to realize that surrender had to do with letting go of my designs for my quiet time. Part of faith was in allowing enough stillness to hear the still, small Voice.

Gradually, I came to recognize that there would always be an agenda item or a problem, but the real task for a retreat was to make contact with God. My primary agenda for a meditation time was to practice the presence of God. He would bring to my mind and heart the things *He* wanted for that period, and so I learned to surrender even the time to Him.

Sometimes, I am quite surprised by the agenda God sets, and this Concho River afternoon provided just that sort of experience. God used the silence of that day and the warm contentment in His presence to apply the truths of my current Bible study to my most important human relationship, *my marriage.*

For the previous seven months, I had been teaching the Sermon on the Mount to the Ladies' Thursday morning Bible Study at our church. When I teach, I spend as much time contemplating practical applications of the truths as I do researching the facts of the text. It is critically important to me that the principles of the Scripture relate to real life, and so I take the current study as seeds for contemplation on my regular walks, while I run my car pools, and as I carry on the realities of family life.

There on the bank of the river, it was as if God put the principles of the Sermon on the Mount up against the reality of my marriage. As if God was right there removing the scales from my eyes, I began to see how the expectations and fantasies I had held for marriage, as fantastic as they were, weren't nearly good enough to match up with the kind of life-style presented in Jesus' teachings. "Can your marriage square up with my teachings?" seemed to be the probing question of the day.

What was I going to do with Jesus' teachings about anger and forgiveness? How did "agreeing with my adversary quickly" work when it seemed that my husband was the adversary? Surely, that injunction applied only to disagreements out in the marketplace and not over the checkbook or the dividing up of household chores!

How did the worry and judging and criticism fit with Jesus' clear directions about these issues? If I quit plucking the specks from Martus's eyes, who would? Perhaps the teachings of Jesus were just for the "spiritual" life and didn't really have anything to do with the realities of marriage. After all, marriage in Jesus' day was different from these days of liberated thinking.

And what about that "going the second mile" business? Could that really work in a marriage? How did that fit with the world's insistence that I get my needs met? Weren't there some areas in which going the second mile wouldn't work? Could I really go the second mile and maintain those precious personal boundaries? What about the danger of taking advantage of each other?

I tried all sorts of ways to outfox the truth with my excuses and game-playing. Try as I would, however, I couldn't get away from the conviction that my growing edge in prayer and meditation was in the stuff of my marriage. My brokenness as a human being and as a Christian was to be healed as I continued on the sacred journey of marriage, with the marriage itself as a unique pathway to wholeness for the partners.

It had bothered me that I didn't have perfect peace within my marriage. I thought that the fact that there were any problems between Martus and me meant that something was "wrong" with us or with the marriage. So, in my fear that something was wrong, I hid from facing problems and solving conflicts. I didn't realize that the very things that evoked the conflicts were the instruments of Christ's healing love. I didn't know that the broken places that marriage exposed offered the greatest opportunities for growth—but I was to learn.

It was as clear to me as the spring blue sky, that Jesus Christ Himself was coming to me within the context of my marriage. My marriage was, in a way, a crucible, in which the two of us were being held near the refining fire of Christ's love. Christ Himself was present between us, attempting to bring forth redemption for each of us through the marriage.

"What *is* the difference between regular marriage and spiritual marriage?" I kept asking in later days. Several friends made attempts to satisfy my questions, but nothing quite quenched my curiosity.

"A spiritual marriage is one in which couples pray together, read the Bible, and attend church together," was the answer of some. I knew statistics showed that couples who do those things together often show a greater level of commitment to stay in a marriage. I understood that involvement in a religious community of faith could act as a deterrent to divorce.

I kept wondering, however, about the absence of joy in so many of the marriages between Christians. Could it be, I wondered, that simply doing the rituals would insure a "spiritual" marriage? Those unchurched couples who seemed so close and happy together nagged at my mind, as well as those who attend church and make each other's lives a living hell. It couldn't be that meeting the externals of Christianity would do it.

"A spiritual marriage is one in which both partners are in recovery," Kara, a friend in a Twelve Step group, told me. "It's when you can share your deepest feelings."

When one partner begins a journey of recovery or growth, the entire marriage is set spinning. Consequently, many couples divorce when the dynamics of growth and change set in. However, when the partners can approach the change by seeing that even their *relationship* can be "in recovery," there is an element of spirituality set loose.

I decided, however, that neither the ability to work a recovery program with a relationship nor the willingness to express feelings necessarily qualifies a marriage as spiritual. Nor is it the amount of self-knowledge or communication skills that gives a marriage that spark of spirituality.

I hold a most unpleasant memory of a seminar with a couple who could go through all the motions of communication training but had an underlying competitiveness and anger with each other that could not be hidden under a glossy exterior. It was as if they knew all the right things to say, and they said them well, but the underlying hostility between them screamed so loudly that we could barely hear the actual words they were saying.

As always when I take my questions and puzzlements into my meditation time, God eventually showed me the answer. As I prayed about my own marriage, I decided that a spiritual marriage, and more specifically a Christian marriage, is one in which the partners are willing to incarnate Christ to each other. Miracles take place between spouses when there is a willingness to express the nature of Christ to each other.

The willingness to incarnate Christ to each other takes the form of servanthood within the marriage, but that servanthood

132

emerges out of the primary relationship with Christ. Incarnating Christ to each other is about loving out of strength and not out of co-dependence. It is about laying down one's life for one's mate in a myriad of ways; it is not about being a doormat. Incarnational love cannot happen apart from communion with Christ any more than branches can produce grapes if they are separated from the vine.

"We could talk about everything before we got married, but now we can't seem to find anything to say and we even avoid being together." Linda and Jay echoed countless newlyweds who couldn't figure out what happened to put the lid on the easy intimacy of their courtship. They were discovering the old Garden of Eden trick: When afraid, sew on fig leaves of defense to protect yourself from being seen and known!

In their outstanding book *Do I Have to Give Up Me to Be Loved by You?* Jordan and Margaret Paul address the instinctive urge to protect oneself within the jarring closeness of marriage. The world's way is to run and hide behind defenses of all kinds, so that brides and grooms often wonder what changed from the marriage ceremony to the honeymoon, or from the honeymoon to the first year's anniversary.

A look at the life of Jesus gives a picture of His willingness to be vulnerable, which grew out of His security in knowing the source of His life. Likewise, spouses can live into the evolving nature of their marriage as they gain their identity and strength from ongoing communion with the Father. The presence of the Divine Third is nowhere more helpful than in the intimacy of marriage.

A spiritual marriage is one in which the natural fear of closeness and vulnerability of intimacy is faced straight on. There is a willingness to allow the fear to exist, and to acknowledge that it is a part of loving at that level. There is an acceptance of the discomfort and uncertainty that comes in the close-range contact of marriage, and a commitment to remain openhearted even in the presence of pain.

When both partners surrender to the activity of Jesus Christ's living and loving presence, change takes place. When both partners recognize and value the presence of Christ within the other, and when there is an effort to live out the teachings of Christ within the relationship, the marriage truly takes on that spiritual dimension.

Harville Hendrix, therapist, educator, and author of the bestselling book *Getting the Love You Want*, defines a "conscious" marriage, and that definition seems to parallel the characteristics of a spiritual marriage. Within a marriage, it is the pain that often jolts the partners into awareness and consciousness, just as the pain of his choices forced the prodigal son to "come to his senses."

Those who choose to stay asleep within a marriage are choosing to stay emotionally dead and to ignore problems. That choice also paves the way for an emotional (and often actual) divorce. Choosing to open up to the pain of the marriage opens up the possibility of healing.

The world's pattern of marriage often sees the marriage as a business arrangement, negotiating the responsibilities and terms as one might a corporate merger. In a worldlike marriage, the focus is on my needs versus your needs, and a competitive spirit overpowers a cooperative one. In the most insidious trap of the world's way of being married, spouses too often give up when the going gets tough.

A spiritual marriage, on the other hand, provides numerous opportunities to "carry each other's burdens" (Galatians 6:2). That quality of faithfulness—which, more than simply avoiding adultery, is an active participation in the healing of each other—often puts us on the razor's edge of pain. That pain, however, pierces us, awakens us.

I have discovered that Christ comes to me not as I try to change or run away from the struggles with my husband, but as I participate with him in them. Indeed, the willingness to remain open to the problem and bear each other's burdens invites us into the next phase of growth.

Refusing the traps of the ego when it tries to pull us back into isolation, but choosing to walk love's great balance beams, is a great deal like following Christ's command to His disciples who had fished all night to no avail. "Cast on the other side," He told them, encouraging them to "go deeper." Casting on the side of courage and willingness, being willing to go deeper into the relationship, yields a bounty of blessings.

This bearing of each other's burdens is not taking on the other's responsibility or taking the blame for each other's burdens. It is not doing for another what he must do for himself. It is not allowing myself to be hooked by others' character defects, reacting to them in self-defeating ways.

Bearing my husband's burdens means that I am affected by his pain, his faults, and his challenges, and he is affected by my brokenness. His character defects and faults impact me in specific ways, but I am not destroyed by those things, because the source of my worth lies in my relationship with God. Bearing his burdens means that I do not allow his fear to engulf me, his anger to stifle my love, or his self-centeredness to evoke my self-centeredness. Indeed, only as I face my husband's brokenness and learn to live with his unique faults do I find healing for some of my own brokenness.

Bearing Martus's burdens means that I don't abandon him emotionally or literally when he fails in his work or fails to meet me halfway. It means that I encourage him when he is down instead of getting down and wallowing with him in despair. It means that I respond to what is poor and hungry and needy and unlovely in him as Christ has responded to what is outcast in me.

I cannot love that kind of love without the presence of Christ

135

infusing my own life. I cannot, of my own power, bear my husband's pain unless I am yielding my own pain to the Great Physician. Without my conscious contact with God, I can play my rescuing and controlling games and think I am bearing his burdens. But with that conscious contact with God, I can see the difference between Martus and me.

Without relational praying, I play the role of enabler in my marriage, getting enmeshed in Martus's problems. With praying, I am empowered by God's liberating spirit and can transcend the difficulties of living together. Resting in the Lord, continuing to surrender the problems of my marriage to Him instead of assaulting the problems with my own solutions, builds strength and creates peace. It is all an issue of making *first things first.*

This giving up of my preconceived expectations is part of dying to myself. Over and over, I recognize the places where I am trying to squeeze some part of life into the tight mold of my needs and wants. I try to make life and the people in my life look just like the pictures I carry in my head of how things *should* be.

My fantasies about marriage were pretty typical of a person who had come of age in the sixties. I bought into the expectations of my culture that insisted that marriage was no longer an economic or social necessity but was for fulfilling deep needs for intimacy. In over ten years of leading Marriage Enrichment Retreats, Couples' Communication, and Bi/Polar Seminars, Martus and I learned a great many techniques.

Furthermore, I knew so much! Hadn't I devoured countless books on getting all the love you need and lighting somebody's fire? Didn't others know that in my office they could find filing cabinets filled with exercises, techniques, and tricks for making love happen?

The only problem was that I was so focused on forcing this marriage to live up to my expectations that I was missing what the relationship could be. In my need to "be perfect," I strove to have the best marriage of all. I expected this one fallible, human husband to be best friend, soul mate, playmate, wise counselor, as well as a Perfect Father/Mother nurturer, and I would be perfection to him as well.

I was at a crossroads, then, on the bank of the Concho River. I was about to be set on a journey of radical change. My meditation had been cracking the hard facade of my ego and stripping away my arrogance, preparing me for a new depth of loving. In those quiet moments, memories of past efforts, failures, mistakes gently bubbled up into my conscious mind to show me that the presence of Christ would take the struggles of the past years and make something brand-new. Suddenly, I saw that the past was prelude; the inner work that had been going on was about to take on new meaning within the intimacy of marriage.

I suppose I cling to my fantasies to keep myself from knowing that I don't know how to do something. Those mental pictures serve as a protection from the awareness that I am into something bigger than I am. For a moment I can forget that I am scared to death of failure, especially within something as important as marriage.

"I should know how to do better than this," was a constant message I gave myself about marriage. I went into the most significant relationship of my life thinking that I knew how to carry it off. I had, after all, given a great deal of thought to what I wanted in a marriage. I had ideas about how my husband would treat me and what he would do for me. I had no patience with the advice I was given before I married (or after, for that matter), for mine would be the perfect marriage.

As the inevitable disillusionments came, my self-will hardened and deepened. As I became more and more aware of my insufficiencies in being close, I couldn't acknowledge that I was, after all, only human and was participating in a relationship that has the greatest potential for pain and suffering (as well as joy and delight). Unable to live as a little child, I beat myself for what I didn't know and for what I couldn't seem to do.

When I wasn't working myself over for my failures in being close, I would blame a problem on Martus. *If only Martus would do what I told him to do,* I thought, *everything would be fine. If only I could get him to read my mind and meet my expectations and fill my need, we would be in great shape!*

The force that gave stability to my marriage has always been a deep commitment to the marriage (which is different from being committed to a person). What that really meant was that I had no intention of giving up! When being close became difficult, I would, by my self-will and cunning, either flee or fight. When my need for power and freedom were at odds with my need for belonging, I would grit my teeth and read another book on getting along. I was determined not to fail.

My meditation through the years, however, was the key in bringing me to this awakening moment in the tender days of spring. The presence of Christ would show me how to love at this most significant human level of all, just as that presence had led me to see the destructiveness of my willfulness.

In those moments by the river, my memory gave me a tour of the past years. I saw, for the first time, that my spiritual quest had created a tension between my earthly attachments and my attachment to God. I saw that I was still holding on to marriage as an idol and to my husband as a god.

The longer I sat quiet, the more clearly I could see that God had been at work, getting my attention through the marriage itself, making the marriage a teacher, a guide, and an instrument of His own. I saw that the disillusionments within the marriage, those recognitions of reality, were actually gifts from God, moving me from depending on earthly resources to yielding to the only dependence that would bring peace.

By God's grace, I saw that the "suffering" I experienced within the closeness of marriage, that grating of one self-will against another, was the result of my desiring something or someone more than God. It was time to get priorities in sync with God's intent. Prayer had led me to the awareness, and now it would lead me to the next step of wholeness.

I felt profoundly touched that day, and what I really wanted to do was rush home and assault Martus with my experience. I wanted to tell him about the flood of awarenesses that had come to me, unbidden. More than anything else, I longed for him to see how much I had changed, just by that encounter on the riverbank—and then, of course, he would change as well. My sharing of my spiritual high would surely turn us around, and we would finally have that spiritual marriage I wanted.

Past experience had tempered my response to these moments, however. I knew that insight didn't mean change. I also knew that my hurry to tell Martus was a symptom of a tendency I have to slough off my responsibility onto him. If I shared my transforming moment with him, then he would surely pick up the ball and run with it, and I would be off the hook. Something—or Someone—told me, on the way home, that this was *my* growth challenge and my journey. While the message was for the marriage, it was about my part in the marriage, and it was crucial for my spiritual growth that I do my part of the work.

I needed to ponder these thoughts in my heart before I put them out for discussion. These insights were so tender and the revelations so personal that they needed the protection of a gestation period. In the fullness of time, action and change would be born, but it was not time for that. My encounter on the river called for more praying.

In my meditation time, then, I offered my relationship with Martus to God. Over and over, still, I see myself standing with Martus before Christ, and that process never fails to reveal truth. I cannot, in my mind's eye, stand before Christ and not see my own part in the problems. When I continue to surrender the relationship to God, He always provides mercy and grace, as well as practical guidance, in one form or another. I have learned not to fret about when or where or how it will come, but I have come to know with assurance that it will come.

The Spirit of Christ reveals the places I am hiding. He shows me where I am playing the victim or the scapegoat, taking more responsibility or blame than is mine in an attempt to protect Martus. As I become more dependent on my Heavenly Father, He shows me the times when I try to force Martus to play a parental role. He shows me the places where I don't want to grow up and be an adult, preferring to remain immature and childish.

"You marry the person who will cause you the greatest discomfort," the counselor told me. She was giving me a review of a seminar she had attended. Little did she know that her comment would dog me for weeks.

I couldn't deny that it seems as though few couples find real contentment with each other. I recognize that the primary problem in marriages is often a conflict of interests, values, and personalities. I know all about how opposites attract and then immediately start trying to change each other. I have seen enough marriages go sour in my day to know that marriage is too often a prison instead of a party.

Perhaps, I thought, the counselor's revelation helped explain the fact that people who divorce often wind up marrying the same type of person again. Over and over, people create the same kinds of relationships with eerie predictability. Maybe what the counselor said was true.

Although my first reaction to the statement was resistance, I knew I needed to ponder its message. If that is true, I asked myself, how does any marriage survive? Why do we do that to ourselves anyway? If it is true that we marry people in order to resolve childhood conflicts, is it possible that by closing emotional doors to each other or by running from one relationship to another, we are failing our most important exams?

In a very real way, marriage offers the most profound arena in which to live out the call of Christ. Because of its ability to expose character defects and the littleness of each other, it also provides an opportunity for running from each other. The deeper the relationship, the more potential there is for pain, but there is also the corresponding opportunity to face those very things that distort the image of God within us and between us.

Since making a home together triggers all sorts of memories and feelings about one's home of origin, there are natural tendencies to project onto the marriage the feelings about that first family. It seems that most couples instinctively create the same dynamics that they learned in their homes of origin, often playing out the very part they had most wanted to avoid.

The liberating truth is that, by allowing the problem and by working through it, the marriage grows. The couple's greatest weakness can be the very thing that makes the marriage strong, just as a person's greatest pain or failure can be his touchstone to victory.

Indeed, it seems as if there is something about us that does draw us together with those who provide learning experiences for us. I have come to understand that running away from those experiences thwarts the growth that God wants. Working through the problem and allowing God to use that problem, then, becomes the way He extends grace, while running away is a failure of one of the main tests of our lives!

The easiest person to be with may not be the person meant for you, and perhaps that myth of the "perfect person who will meet my needs" is one of the greatest disservices of our culture. The media images that feed us, whether we are aware of them or not, seep into our hearts and make us dissatisfied with each other's imperfections.

Perhaps, too, that holding on to the myths within marriage is one of the ways we conform to the world, for that idea of mythical perfection seduces us with promises of instant gratification, constant comfort, quick fixes, and a pain-free existence. Those easy streets of the world seduce the best of us into dissatisfaction with the realities of flesh-and-blood living. The myths promoted by our culture perpetuate a narcissism that eats away at the possibility of real loving.

Martus Miley's practical nature has both frustrated me and made me wake up to the reality of the bottom line. His quietness has driven me mad and forced me to get acquainted with the quietness within my own soul. I have tried to change Martus's reservedness and his mind, only come up against my need to control others' moods and temperaments. I have tried to get him to meet my needs in my way only to discover that there are some needs I have to meet on my own. The most distressing discovery of all has been that I cannot play God in his life any more than I can make him be my God and get by with it.

The truth is that I am married to my perfect spiritual partner. I am married to the person I need to be married to, and the resistance I experience comes when I expect the marriage to be comfortable and painless.

Through the years of Marriage Enrichment Retreats, Martus and I have come to use several metaphors to describe this delicate relationship of love. We talk about how deadly the concept of "settling down" is to a marriage. We encourage couples to see the relationship as a ship, setting out on a great voyage—and everybody knows that voyages incur storms.

"She just doesn't love me" or "He doesn't love me the way I want him to" are the plaintive moanings of human beings who are caught in the traps of the world's view of what a marriage should be. "She (or he) simply doesn't meet my needs" is the sour tune of the child who is old enough to take a marriage vow but still unwilling to grow up.

Another metaphor we use for marriage centers on the idea that marriage is a wonderful box of delicacies from which each partner can pick and choose whatever treats he wants. Actually, marriage is an empty box, and both partners fill it with all kinds of experiences and responsibilities.

My favorite metaphor, however, is that the marriage is the first child of the union, and that it grows and develops as it is tended and nurtured from infancy on into maturity. No one expects a newborn baby to give what a mature adult can. Nor do we expect a baby to thrive without nourishment. So it is with a marriage. As the marriage is given time, love, care, attention, it will eventually give back to the participants.

Just as God has a design for each individual, He also has an idea of how He wants marriage to be. Within the context of relational prayer, of allowing the Divine Third to be the Designer and Builder of the marriage, the marriage is able to grow through the various stages of development to become what God intended it to be.

When one or both of the partners places God first, love is set free and the partner is able to grow within the marriage. With the awareness of the presence of God, it is possible to see beyond the actions and words (the externals) of a person to the spirit of the person. With the eyes of love, it is possible to see that person as he really is, and then the need to make him into a god vanishes. Receiving Christ's love in that first relationship frees the individual to move beyond seeking to get his own needs met to a willingness and a desire to meet the other's needs, to love the other out of a centeredness in Christ's love rather than to get love from the other.

When couples are attuned to Christ's presence, there is a communication beyond mere words. There is the power to overcome differentness and separation, to lay down defensiveness, to solve problems, and to see with the mind of God. With Christ at the center, real acceptance and celebration of each other's uniqueness is possible. When that happens, the marriage becomes a source of infinite strength and creativity.

Therefore, the most important aspect of marriage is seeking first the presence of Christ within the individual life. When I do that, I have what I need to carry on the fragile dance of separateness and togetherness, of coming together and moving apart in the relationship, which has the potential of giving the greatest amount of joy and peace and love. Marriage, lived out before God, becomes an instrument of divine peace.

A spiritual marriage, then, is a marriage of durable love, withstanding and transcending love. It both requires and gives the willingness to accept the pain of closeness without closing off one's heart to the other. It is a relationship of openheartedness, of willingness, of graciousness.

A spiritual marriage is one of giving love rather than demanding love, and that emerges only out of communion with the greatest Lover of all. Marriage holds the potential for being that safe place, a sanctuary, a place of deep communion. Marriage at its best is one of God's greatest channels of His love.

10
A Little Child Shall Lead Them

Then to receive a child in the name of Jesus is to receive Jesus; to receive Jesus is to receive God; therefore to receive the child is to receive God himself.

—George MacDonald

Do not embitter your children, or they will become discouraged.

Colossians 3:21

———◦◦◦———

"What's the matter, didn't she let you sleep last night?" Elaine asked knowingly, holding back a laugh. Her first child was already two years old, but I was just beginning to make my way through the perilous waters of parenting. I had a sneaking suspicion that my carefree youth was over.

Overnight, I learned that this "helpless" infant wielded total control over three adults—her mother and father and, thankfully, her wiser and more experienced grandmother. Within the first few hours of her homecoming, that seven-pound person let us know that her very presence in our lives would necessitate change.

"I had a friend whose baby didn't sleep over two hours at a time for the first year," Elaine continued. One day, the exhausted mother finally got the baby to sleep and went in to take a nap herself. Just as her eyes closed, the baby began crying, and the desperate young mother wailed, "I can't take it! I've got twenty-one years of no sleep ahead of me!"

Elaine's story brought into sharp focus something I had begun to suspect but wanted to avoid knowing. For the first time in my life, I had gotten into something bigger than I was. What had seemed a sweet and exciting idea had turned into an overwhelming responsibility. I was definitely going to be changed by parenting. My love for this beautiful, tiny, dependent bundle of potential would be a refining fire like no other.

I had no idea how much parenting would make me grow. Every single stage of development of each one of my three children demands a change in me. Their growing edges slice across my own life, exposing my own jagged edges of imperfection and inadequacy. However, my children are also instruments of incredible grace and growth. Parenting is another of the great paradoxes of love.

Elaine's story is symbolic for the awakening that parenting forces. The truth of the matter is that parenting evokes feelings and impulses I never imagined. It creates pain and joy I could never have anticipated. Parenting provides numerous opportunities for becoming conscious, or "coming to," and it is a most excellent pathway to becoming whole. The process of loving children into maturity exposes all that is immature and unfinished in the parents. As with marriage, and as with spiritual growth, parenting forces a choice of how to live.

I began parenting with a deep desire that each child would feel valued and heard. Although I wasn't really clear about what all that meant, I wanted my children to feel that they and their vote were important to me. I felt a strong need to be their guide and support, an encourager to emerging personalities. My idealism led me to believe that surely there was some model of parenting that fell somewhere between the extremes of permissivism and authoritarianism.

B.C. (Before Children), I could hardly wait to fill the role of "Mother." I had planned out in my mind what I would be and do and say as a mother. I would be teacher, counselor, provider, nurse, and storyteller. I would bake cookies and listen to their stories and dispense wisdom and knowledge, which they would eagerly take—for, after all, I would be such a *good mother*. In my mind's eye, I had inexhaustible patience and unlimited time to meet whatever need that child might have.

In those early days of parenting, I would sit in the rocker, especially bought and prepared just for rocking the baby, nursing my beautiful newborn. I kept a low table by that chair (I had read about that in one of the books on "preparing for baby"), and on that table I kept the "right" toys to stimulate that child at different stages of her development.

There were two stacks of books on that table, too. Picture books appropriate for the earliest months held touchy-feely pages and bright, primary colors. The other stack was for me, and it contained numerous parenting books, which I would read as I rocked my infant.

To my mother's eternal credit, she didn't laugh at me. She, who had helped numerous infants get a good start on this planet, exhibited infinite patience with this neophyte mother who wanted desperately to "do it right." I can only imagine what she must have thought as I rocked and read "the authorities."

Perhaps she remembered how much she wanted to "do it right" when she first started. Maybe she could remember being overwhelmed by the responsibility of a brand-new life. Perhaps she had learned what I was to learn, that parenting is a lifelong adventure in letting go. In not making fun of my efforts, she was letting go of her own child. I think she knew, as well, that this newborn life would be my teacher in ways I could not, at this point in my own newbornness, imagine.

This winter, nearly twenty years later, a new picture of my three teenagers sits in my bedroom. They are lovely young ladies now, smiling brightly at me from a flowered frame. As I look at their fresh, eager faces, I am appalled to recall the arduous effort it has taken to get them to this place. Most of all, I am overwhelmed by the awareness that, in my seeking to parent consciously and cooperatively, I have encountered both their willfulness and their strength. In respecting who each child is, I have discovered who I am.

Each one of them has been my teacher. Together and separately, they have provided intense and frequent opportunities for spiritual growth from the moment they were born. Each one has precipitated numerous crises for me, and their growth has called for me to reach far down inside myself for strength I didn't know I had. Each one has been used by God as a means of bringing wholeness to me.

"These chapters on marriage and parenting are eating my lunch," I told my husband as we made our way along icy streets for a lunchtime date, a regular practice we guard carefully against the assaults of our schedules. "The more I write, the more I face my failures and imperfections."

"The ideal is always in conflict with the actual," he told me, and I relaxed into the warmth of the car and the love of his long-term friendship. "But we must keep looking at the ideal and attempt to move toward it."

Because Martus knows me best, and because he knows my worst, too, I was afraid he might tell me I didn't have any business writing about what I couldn't do . . . perfectly. Because Martus knows my failures, I feared his reminding me of those very imperfections I try not to face. Instead, his gentle words became grace to me, and I heard in the voice of my partner his belief in my desire to love well.

I recalled that little piece of needlepoint that says, "God couldn't be everywhere at once, and that is why He made mothers." While I question the theology of the stitchery—and, even more, I resist that pressure our culture places on the mother to be deity to her children—I pondered again the fact that we are to stand in God's stead in nurturing the young. Perhaps that awesome responsibility is the source of much of the pressure of the process.

Perhaps it is the standards of parenting in Christ's love that make me so aware of falling short of His intent. In parenting, the very foundations of my patterns and habits are shattered, so I find that I must intentionally draw on the presence of the Living Christ. Only by His Spirit am I able to carry out my responsibility in loving the tender lives He has loaned me.

Through relational praying and through the accompanying awakening to the realities of being human, I saw that, as much as I wanted to be a perfect parent, I could not be. As much as I wanted to do it right, I would fail. By God's grace, I finally came to terms with the fact that I hurt my children, and they hurt me. I fail and they fail, and we learn together, in the laboratory of home and family, what it means to forgive each other.

There is something about the laundry that evokes my demons and makes me forget the ideals I want to meet. Clothes strewn on the floor can instantaneously erase any remembrance of the high and holy hour of the quiet time I just had. After a verbal battle with one of my children, I am left to wonder how a child's words can hook the petulant child in me so that we both get involved in a battle of wills and wind up acting like spoiled brats. What is it about a little child that can set off rage and fury in a full-grown adult?

There is something about a teenager's mood swings that can turn a household into a minefield, with the only certainty being that there *will* be an explosion. Sometimes, the choices that my children make can make me forget all about faith. I hate to admit it, but there are times when what is going on between one of my girls and a boyfriend can wreak havoc in my marriage. What rationale do I use, unconsciously, to convince myself that how my children perform is a reflection on my parenting?

Part of the blessing of prayer is that the presence of Christ heals those memories of times I hurt my child. Christ's grace helps me deal with the guilt over my failures, the sorrow over the times when I fell short of what I knew was right with the people I treasure most. Through the strengthening that comes in prayer, I find the courage to be honest about my own faults. Modeling honesty can only help my children avoid excusing their own character defects and failures by hiding behind the skirts of my imperfection.

"The hardest thing for me to do is to come down from that pulpit," my husband tells our church, "and go home to live what I have just preached."

Parenting sends a man and a woman out to dance upon the razor's edge of risk, challenging us to confront the disparity between what we know to do and what we can do. Prayer has led me to give up my unrealistic expectations about who I am called to be as a human parent. It has also freed me to see each child as an individual, autonomous creation of God instead of the *object* of my parenting skills.

As with other relationships, but perhaps more intensely within the parent-child dynamics, peace and joy are blurred or destroyed in direct proportion to the "shoulds" and "should nots" we place upon ourselves as parents. The expectations some of us hold for ourselves in meeting the needs of our children are expectations only God Himself can meet.

I heard Proverbs 22:6 quoted all of my life. "Train a child in the way he should go," it says, "and when he is old he will not turn from it." What great assurance those words have been for earnest and sincere parents who have thought that they could, like Job, put a big enough hedge around their children by insisting on church attendance and Scripture memory to protect them from all the assaults of the world. What comfort parents through the ages have taken in that Scripture, thinking that while things might be terrible now with a rebellious child, *eventually* that child would return to the "right" things.

The only problem is that, too often, children who grew up within the strict and constant care of Mother Church don't want to darken its doors anymore. There are too many examples of fine, upstanding, good parents who kept every letter of the law, only to see their offspring spit in the face of everything that the family holds dear.

The challenge comes in seeing that the real meaning of that Scripture has to do with encouraging and nurturing the child *to become who God intended him to be*. The task, as parents, is to discern what traits and potentialities God designed into that unique, separate, and autonomous human being, as opposed to forcing that child to fit into the mold of our expectations. A parent is to accept and embrace who that child is, and then help the child become all he was created to be.

"I'm not you, Mom," one of my girls told me recently. "I need to make my own choices." I had to admit that she was right, but how hard it is for me to trust that much!

Without that respect and reverence due my child, my self-centered will and my fear-based ego seduce me into thinking that my child exists to meet my needs, to fulfill my dreams and desires, to perform according to my mental images of how a good child should treat his parents. Without that sense of Christ's convicting presence, I miss the fact that my child is often the instrument of Christ's healing touch in my life. Without the transforming friendship with Christ, I forget that it is *the child who is my teacher*, and that I am teaching him what I am trying to learn.

Everything about my parenting changes when I see the process as *participating with God* in nurturing one of His creations. I take a totally different approach when I understand that my child is accountable, ultimately, to his Heavenly Parent, and not to me. That knowledge takes the pressure of performance, of "doing it right," of bringing up the perfect child and throws it to the wind. It also frees me to parent, led and guided by the wind of God's Spirit.

The challenge of parenting my own children in this culture calls for my awareness of Christ's participating presence both within my children and in the spaces between us. I have come to believe that Jesus Christ longs for each parent to be in a state of "at-one-ment" with Him, and for the parenting to emerge out of that divine friendship.

Out of that sense of Christ's presence, I have come to hold deep respect for each of my children. I have come to honor their differentness from me. I celebrate their sense of their own individuality, nurtured within the warmth of an active, warm (and sometimes heated) family. In prayer, I have come to understand the wisdom of giving both roots and wings, and I know that without divine participation in my parenting, I will do too much of one or not enough of the other. Practicing the presence of Christ helps me to see that each child is God's messenger to me.

In parenting, I come face-to-face every day with the pull of opposing needs for both dependence and independence. While I know that creative parenting emerges out of negotiating the wild currents of these opposing forces, I also know I do that best when I am aligned with God's love. So prayer is absolutely the most essential ingredient of my parenting. It is prayer that keeps me balanced between the extremes of parenting styles.

"Children step on your feet when they are little, but on your heart when they grow up." The mother of four grown children gave me a preview of the parenting of adult children, and I resisted her words with everything in me. Didn't she know that I was working hard to avoid being hurt by my children? Couldn't she tell that I was going to build a hedge big enough to avoid that pitfall?

My sister's mother-in-law would say, when complimented on her sons, who are the epitome of goodness, "Oh, thank you, but you know that they aren't dead yet, and anything can happen!" We loved to laugh about her obvious humility and sense of reality, but our laughter is interspersed with the awareness that, because there is so much at stake in parenting, there is a tremendous potential for pain. Choosing to love as a parent opens up all kinds of possibilities for being hurt.

It is important to face the reality that, while children evoke childhood wounds, they also embarrass and wound us. They keep us humble. Even when they "don't cause us any trouble," meaning that they say no to drugs, sex, and alcohol, there is always the discomfort of sending them out into the world to face the risks and potential calamities from which we wish we could keep them.

Children force us to our knees, which is exactly where God wants us. Children provide all sorts of wonderful opportunities for listening to Him. We create our own pain and are a pain to our children when we pretend that we know it all.

Sometimes, some trait of a child "hooks" the little child within his parent. Often, some long-buried memory of what it was like to be small and dependent on an adult bubbles up from the past to color the present. Sometimes the pain from the family behind shapes the family ahead. That is why family therapists say that knowing a person within three generations provides the best way of understanding him.

Children force the parent to recognize and work with unresolved issues of his own. In that way, a child serves as a conduit of grace, offering an opportunity for inner healing of the parent's wounded little child.

"I keep rushing around, trying to make my child feel secure," the frazzled mother confessed to a spiritual growth group, "but he already feels secure!" She was to find out that her overprotectiveness was an attempt to exorcise some of the fears she had from her own history. The problem was that her children didn't have that same history, and they needed autonomy! By taking the time and effort to walk into her own woundedness, and dealing with her own "stuff" instead of trying to work it out through her children, she found healing.

"I don't want my children to have the same kinds of burdens I did. I had to grow up too fast." The sadness in Jeffrey's face revealed a wounded inner child, but instead of submitting that part of himself to the healing power of Christ's love, he was attempting to do for his children what had not been done for him. Consequently, Jeffrey's children were not learning about reasonable responsibility.

"Prayer has helped me take my eyes off the abuses of my childhood," Alex told us in a session on prayer and meditation. "Now, when those old, harmful memories come up, I see Christ standing there with me, when I was six." Gradually, the pain of his past is being healed, and he is gaining the courage to get close to his children, whom he had held at a distance out of fear of repeating the patterns of his past.

Sometimes, too, there is a child whom the parent cannot accept, or a trait in a child that you've been sure you would never tolerate. There are those children who seem to be the incarnation of a relative you cannot stand. Some remind you of one of your own weaknesses.

"My youngest son is my mother-in-law made over," one of the members of a group told us, "and I feel as defeated in dealing with him as I did with her."

Carol found she had a chance to relearn a lesson she had failed with her mother-in-law, whom she had avoided at all costs. This new lesson in its updated version in the younger generation was about readjusting her expectations of someone with a different temperament. She was also getting powerful, but painful, lessons in letting go of control and facing problems head-on. Carol found that solving the problem with the generation in front of her also brought healing with the generation behind her. The lesson she learned with her child also helped her in dealing with other people of his temperament.

Children offer the gift of wholeness to the parent when the parent can identify his own disowned selves. When I let myself see that part of myself that I have rejected or tried to repress—a part that is now popping up in one of my children—I can walk into truth and grace, and then freedom.

"In my imagination," Carol told us, "I picture myself sitting down with my mother-in-law and Christ. I can hear guidance from Christ, and, for the first time, I am getting in touch with the frustrations Mom must have had with me. This relational praying really works!"

"I want my children to look beyond me, their earthly father, to their Heavenly Father," our speaker told us in a workshop on dealing with the stresses of family life. I couldn't have agreed more, but I also couldn't help but wonder about the epidemic tendency to blame one's mother for whatever is wrong. In what was a revolutionary thought for me, I wondered if, perhaps, there needed to be a fleshing out of our concepts about the full nature of God, so that each of us could also become acquainted with God's motherly side.

Those feminine strengths of God are expressed all through Scripture, all the way from the "brooding" over creation in Genesis 1 to the innumerable examples of God's caring, gentle, nurturing, tending presence. The concept of the Heavenly Parent is throughout Scripture but has not been explored in my expression of Christ's church. Perhaps meeting the feminine aspects of the Wholly Other might take some of the pressure off the feminine humans who are burdened down with the unrealistic expectations of what it means in our culture to be "Mother."

"I don't want to talk about it, Mother," Julie told me one night. "Please don't ask me any questions."

Tears streaked her face. Her voice was firm. I could see that she was hurting, and yet I was being asked to leave her alone.

"But don't you know that I have a great imagination, and when you don't tell me what is wrong, I can imagine all sorts of things," I told this independent individual. Julie held her ground and asked me to leave her room.

Respecting autonomy and encouraging independence are all fine-sounding in theory. But given a weeping, but stone-faced, teenager, I threw theories out the window. I forgot all my good intentions about respecting her space and privacy *out of concern for my own welfare*. I was scared because she was upset, and I was willing to violate her individuality (translated: nag her to death) so that I would feel better. I was crossing her boundaries and trespassing in her territory.

This wasn't the first time my need to know had come up against Julie's resistance to tell. It wasn't the first time she and I had stood toe-to-toe in a battle of wills. As I left her room that night, I recalled another, similar encounter when I reminded her of my great imagination. "Well, then, you'll just give your imagination a great workout, won't you?" Julie had replied.

Coming up against the differences in temperament in my children has been a pathway of healing for me. Julie's need for autonomy has done battle with my need to control. Michelle's sense of adventure and her incredible tenacity try my patience and hook my tendencies to smother. Amy's compassion for others and her willingness to suffer with her friends brings up my own compulsion to protect her from being hurt by others.

Parenting is a big job, and it carries stiff responsibilities. However, if I can allow my children to be who they are and to follow the pathway that God opens to them, they will bring great adventure to me. My children will show me parts of the world I might have missed. They will also reveal God to me as He expresses Himself through them.

The point is that the process of parenting exposes areas that need to be offered to the healing hands of Christ. When one of these issues emerges, I need to stay aware enough to let the instance teach me and lead me into the deeper waters of wholeness.

More than anything, each child teaches the parent about letting go—letting go of control and power, of expectations and fantasies. Perhaps the most important surrender of all is when the child teaches the parent to give up dwelling on mistakes and failures and to accept divine forgiveness. Perhaps our children, in their tender words, "It's okay, Mom," teach us best what it is to fail, repent, get up, and start all over again.

"I just realized I came from a dysfunctional family," wept my friend, "and I just can't bear to look at the truth of that."

Who didn't? I couldn't help but think. Who didn't come from a family in which there was brokenness and pain? Is there a family anywhere that doesn't have its areas of denial, its forbidden topics of discussion, its secrets? Where in the world is there a family that is game-free, where each person is autonomous, but loving, and in perfect balance. The question of family life is in *degree* and *kind: How* dysfunctional was it, and in what ways?

Every child gets hurt growing up. That is the nature of life. And every child reaches adulthood with unmet needs and unfulfilled longings for that mythical "perfect parent" who could have (if only she would have) made things easier for the child. Giving up that myth, turning around and forgiving the parent, accepting that your mother and father did the best they *could*, if not the best they knew, all go a long way in healing the inner child. Recognizing that I might not have been the child my parents wanted keeps me conscious and helps me be more tolerant of their imperfections and mine.

The truth is that every child impacts the parent and changes the parent; the question is whether or not we go willingly into the refining fire or fight it. The child who is the most difficult is often our greatest teacher. The most painful growing edge often becomes the wound that brings beauty. God uses our children to show us ourselves, and he uses the pain implicit in parenting as an opportunity to draw us closer into the arms of the Heavenly Parent.

Parenting brings me dramatically to the awareness of the things I cannot change and the need for serenity, wisdom, and courage in doing what I can. In that humiliating process, I have come to understand most poignantly the need for coming as a little child to the Father, with my hands empty and my mind free, and with my heart open to receive the gift of compassion.

"Children always know the truth about how the parents feel about each other," Michelle told me one night as she and I shared a late-night visit after play practice. True to her newborn days, she still comes alive at midnight, and I am still getting reduced sleep!

158

Stunned, I put down my needlepoint and stared into the face of this seventeen-year-old sage. "What do you mean?" I asked, almost afraid to hear her response.

"Oh, you know, Mom. Kids just know. Parents can't hide the truth from them. The trouble with the kids is that their parents don't like each other!"

Michelle went on to relate the story of one of her friends. I barely heard the story, however, so great was my astonishment that my child already knew one of the great truths about family systems.

Michelle was right, and I needed to hear her wisdom. She knew that peace in the individual makes peace in the marriage, and that peace in the marriage makes peace in the family.

Trying to process our conversation and go to sleep at 2:00 A.M., I wondered how my children see our marriage, and how they will remember our home. I pray they will remember home as a sacred place where love covered the pain we inflicted on each other.

11
Partner on the Journey

Personal guidance is necessary so that the radical move-
ments of Christian discipleship will be helped to relate the
inner and outer worlds in a spiritual direction which takes
account of the movement towards human liberation in our
time. Never was spiritual direction more urgently called for
than in the present climate of soul searching.

—Kenneth Leech

No one has ever seen God; but if we love one another, God
lives in us and his love is made complete in us.

1 John 4:12

The (spiritual) director and he who is being directed are both
seekers. They are both parts of a spiritual direction, a current of
spirituality, a divine-human process of relationship.

It was the back booth at the Crystal Confectionery that provided the sanctuary each Friday at 11:00 A.M. Week after week,
my spiritual director would meet me for lunch, holding me to my
commitment to my disciplines, which I had chosen.

She had been down the road in her own spiritual growth,
merging her own journey with the wisdom of the Twelve Steps,
and so she took me, step by step, on my own odyssey. I fought her
sometimes, but most of the time I followed with a sense of divine

rightness. Often, in the delightful surprises of the shared journey, the two of us were struck by a stunning revelation or by an almost tangible awareness of the presence of the Divine Third—yes, even at the Crystal Confectionery. Christ's appearance opened our eyes.

I learned first about spiritual direction in 1979, when Martus and I attended the Church of the Savior in Washington, D.C. As part of the ongoing nurturing of the mission group of the Well-spring Retreat Center, retreatants could request a spiritual director who would correspond with them on a regular basis.

It didn't take me any time to decide that I wanted a guide on this journey of the inner life. Some deep, inner wisdom convinced me that I needed someone wiser and more mature than I was, to give guidance and encouragement along the way. Could that inner prompting have been the Holy Spirit? I think so.

My particular expression of the church leans heavily on the side of the "priesthood of the believer." That is, each person has direct and personal access to God and can communicate one-on-one with God Himself. I hold that view, but I also have come to understand the danger of pushing that view so far that we ignore our need for accountability.

Within my church experience, there is a heavy emphasis on that initial conversion. Thankfully, some in our church are awakening to the crying need for discipleship and for the intentional, deliberate process of maturing in the faith. I shudder when I think of how little education or support many Christians receive when they are attempting to live out a decision to be a Christian in the marketplace.

I grew up within a framework that held a deep suspicion of the confessional booth. Whether it was actually taught, or whether I assumed it to be true, I believed I should not tell anyone else my problems, much less confess my sins to another human being. In that belief is an implicit fear of being known and judged, and that fear leads to isolation and self-condemnation.

Furthermore, the American culture prizes individuality and self-reliance. As in so many areas, our spiritual lives reflect the culture. In West Texas particularly, taking care of oneself, keeping a stiff upper lip, and not bothering others with your problems are the rules. "I can solve this myself!" is a common theme of the pioneer spirit that still threads itself among us, and many live out lives of quiet and lonely desperation out of a fear of breaking those rules of self-governance.

Madeleine L'Engle tells one of my favorite stories of the human need for tangible and visible assistance. Her son, when he was small, was put to bed upstairs and away from his family. "I'm scared," he kept telling his father, putting him through the usual routine of one last drink of water and one more trip to the bathroom.

"Please, somebody, come be with me," the little boy begged. "I'm lonely."

"God is up there with you," the child's father called to him from the bottom of the stairs. A few moments of silence followed, and he thought he had finally won his evening's peace.

"But I need someone with skin on," came the reply. The wisdom of the child won out.

I, too, needed someone with skin on to represent God to me, to explore the deeper issues of the spiritual life in an atmosphere of love and acceptance. While I was doing pretty well at learning the ways of practicing the presence of Christ and of maintaining conscious contact with Him, I needed the interaction of one of His instruments. Just to read books about other contemplatives finally was not enough for me.

To enter into a relationship in which I would receive spiritual guidance and be accountable to someone other than a teacher or employer was a new thing for me, but I was ready for it. While

162

I felt new and strange and vulnerable, opening the intimacy of my prayer life to another human being, I knew it was essential.

In later years, after reading many of the early writers, I came to understand how perilous the journey inward is without a guide. The more I practiced the presence of Christ and the more important and consistent my prayer life became, the more I became aware of forces I didn't understand. Henri Nouwen, in the introduction to Kenneth Leech's book *Soul Friend*, stresses the importance of a spiritual friend or guide, and describes my own experience perfectly.

> When we enter into the presence of God and try to listen obediently to his voice, we can be misled by our own needs and illusions. It is quite easy to think of our own desires as if they were God's will, to see our personal successes as as sign of God's approval, and to interpret our own failures and pains as God's punishment. The good news of the Gospel—that God came to us in a tangible and visible human being: Jesus Christ—enables us to recognize that our way to God is always a human way, and that without a guide our spiritual journey can entangle us in introspective self-preoccupation instead of helping us to become empty for God.

With eagerness, then, I signed up to participate in a program of spiritual direction through the Wellspring Retreat Center. I could hardly wait to see who my director would be. I knew that this relationship would be an important and significant one in my life, but I had no idea the extent of the gift.

My first spiritual director was Dorothy Devers, a beloved member of the Church of the Savior. For months, she wrote detailed responses to my "reports," taking great care to encourage and confront me, to point out areas of growth I might consider and to guide me to the readings that were appropriate for my stage in the journey.

With hindsight, I can see that the geographic distance between this first spiritual director and me was providential. At that stage, I needed the protection of space and time between us. With my fear of being exposed and vulnerable, it was important and helpful to have my first encounter of this kind be one in which I could maintain a level of separateness.

In time, however, as I continued to practice contemplative prayer and the other disciplines of the inner journey, I became restless with this long-distance arrangement. Furthermore, as I made journaling a process of self-discovery, and as I read voraciously whatever I could get my hands on related to spiritual growth and relationships, I encountered still more of those latent forces I needed to face. It was time to face my demons, to look at my dark side, and to name my shadow self.

Throughout my pilgrimage, the right teacher has always appeared at exactly the right time, and different people have fulfilled this role for me at exactly the right moment in my spiritual development. The key has been in my willingness to ask for the specific relationship I needed.

There are many varieties of spiritual guidance available, and it is important to know what you need. Some people prefer to pay for a counselor who will help them sort through the rough waters of their past or present, giving psychological insight. While this type of relationship is very valuable, it is important to note that counseling is different from spiritual direction.

True spiritual direction is a process in which the director, in a sense, stands in God's stead in loving the directee and intentionally brings the God-dimension into the encounters. The spiritual director must listen to the confessions of the one seeking growth, and must listen carefully with his heart. The director's job is to guide the person to see his life and circumstances from God's perspective. That is accomplished through guidance in Bible study or other spiritual reading, prayer, meditation, worship, and service.

The spiritual director must be willing to confront the lies and deceptions of the directee, to point out areas of denial. The director must be willing to walk the delicate tightrope of holding the directee accountable, while also setting him free to be accountable. The director must also be able to extend forgiveness and grace and to recognize the times when the directee may try to pick up that confessed sin one more time.

"How long are you going to ride that horse?" I was stunned. Sandra was all but shouting at me. "We've already taken care of that. Why do you want to keep going back and picking that up? Do you want to stay stuck there?"

Sandra loved me enough to apply patience when it was needed. She also knew when to intervene in my mind games and my ego fits, to jolt me into remembering that I so easily drifted back into the position of "Guilty" instead of living out the exquisite mercy and grace of the Living Christ.

One of the most precious gifts my director gives me is in sharing her own experience with me. When she entrusts her own strivings and failings, somehow, I gain courage. When she is willing to open up her own heart and let me see her vulnerabilities, I experience the healing love of Christ in a profound way.

"Let me tell you of my experience," she told me one day. We sat before a gentle fire, across from each other so that we could look straight into each other's eyes with nothing between. I knew, without asking, that she had prayed for me before I arrived. I knew that she was praying as she listened to me, and I had complete assurance that my soul friend was praying for me between our sessions. When she leaned forward in her chair to tell me of her own woundedness, I knew that we were sitting on holy ground. My director's gift of trust was a critical part of my own healing; her wounds became the healing ointment for my own.

Her willingness to become "broken bread and poured out wine," as Oswald Chambers calls it, fed my soul.

Throughout the weeks and months of our long-term soul friendship, Sandra has been the Good Samaritan to me. With her availability and patience, she has symbolically washed my feet. She has been God's instrument over and over, yielding her own self-will to His to meet me at the point of my need.

Although a "sponsor" in a Twelve Step program is not necessarily a "spiritual director," the Twelve Steps can provide a powerful structure for the spiritual direction process. The steps of recovery may be used as a process for spiritual growth, giving an orderly and time-tested pattern for the work between director and directee.

Because some people in recovery do not identify the "Higher Power" as God, but as their "highest self" or their "inner guide," it is important to define the terms that the Twelve Steps use. I have learned how important it is to know the name of my Higher Power. I have also recognized that if my highest self is the highest power on which I can call, I am in deep trouble.

Part of my work with Sandra has been with the Twelve Steps, as I sought to apply the principles to areas of my life that are out of control or in the control of my self-willed ego. Because of Sandra's history, however, she was vigilant about making sure that we intentionally and consciously brought the presence of Christ into our conversations. She knew well the temptations of letting a program of recovery or a process of self-discovery take the place of a living, dynamic, vital, and personal relationship with Jesus Christ.

"Well, are you any better?" Sandra probes periodically, checking out to see if I am indeed making progress. She weeps with me when I hurt, and she rejoices heartily when I succeed, but she consistently checks to see if I am moving forward and taking action. "It's one thing to talk the talk," she tells me over and over, "but can you walk your talk?" I need that kind of checking in and accountability to keep my spiritual journey vibrant—and honest.

My spiritual director incarnates Christ to me. As she opens herself to be God's instrument in my life, I become willing to let my life be the channel through which God can work, if He chooses.

Part of the genius of the Twelve Step program is in the Twelfth Step. I call it the evangelism step, and Sandra shudders, but I insist that "telling another hungry beggar where he can find bread" is a profound method of evangelism. It seems that the founders of Alcoholics Anonymous had the good sense, experience, and wisdom to know that you keep something only by giving it away.

One of the joys of my life is in standing in God's stead in loving others, and it has been through those week-by-week appointments with other seekers that I have been forced to rely on the indwelling presence. In listening to the yearnings of empty hearts and the questionings of others, I have faced some of my own yearnings and my own questions and have been forced to turn to the Source of the answers for guidance. Truly, "in giving, I have received."

"Who do I think I am to be a spiritual director?" I kept asking myself and Martus. "I don't have a theology degree," I said, trying to get out of such a serious responsibility. No matter how long I work with others in this process of spiritual growth, I don't ever feel qualified to do it, and I approach the meetings with a sense of awe.

Somehow, though, people with questions about God, about who He is and what He has to do with the pain and suffering of modern life, kept showing up in my living room. The more they showed up, the more I realized my limitations.

I began reading and studying the practice of spiritual direction through the centuries. I made sure that I stayed in a relationship with my own director, so that I was accountable in specific areas in my own journey. If my call, which I had stated at the retreat at the Church of the Savior, was, in fact, to be an instrument of reconciling people to God, and people to each other, then I'd better get serious about preparing myself to live out that call.

"This person is in a serious crisis," I told Martus one evening after I had received a request from a woman who wanted spiritual direction. "Her family is falling apart and she's not even sure she believes there is a God. What can I give her?"

"Be with her. Be her friend," he said. "Presence is the greatest gift of all."

I have learned that, and I have learned that presence is more important than advice. Those who want to be rescued often want advice (which they don't intend to follow!), while those who are serious seekers of God's presence want a place in which they feel safe enough to ask the questions of their hearts. A person who really wants to grow wants encouragement to know his own truth, to listen to his own heart, and to honor his own wisdom. A true disciple of Christ wants human presence and love as he enters into his own one-on-one friendship with the Living Christ.

Through the years, I have discovered that God uses imperfect, broken vessels as His eyes and hands and ears and feet, and I have discovered that walking with another human being in his own process of spiritual growth is a precious privilege. The opportunity to participate in the healing process of another's life has been the instrument of healing in my own life. To facilitate, by presence and by questions, the encounter of an individual with God is to meet God between us in a powerful way.

"I don't know about this Jesus stuff," was the challenge tossed to me one day by a person new to spiritual direction. "I believe in God, but I just don't know about Jesus. That all seems pretty radical to me."

In introducing the presence of the Living Christ to others, I have been profoundly touched by that presence myself. Exploring the ways and means of that Christ in the history of others, I have found His tender ways in my own life. Practicing the presence of Christ with those who do not believe in it, I have been forced to the end of my ability and adequacy, and there, on that razor's edge of risk, I have been moved by *His* complete adequacy.

"Can you see me for spiritual direction," was the request through the phone lines one Thursday afternoon when I felt depleted and empty. I felt as though I had given until I could not give anymore. There was something about this plea, however, that made me carve out the time.

As I sat in the late afternoon and listened to the questions and yearnings of a seeking heart, I felt my energy begin to rise. Speaking of the faithfulness of God, as I had experienced it, somehow was like receiving a blood transfusion. Witnessing to the Light that I knew, the Love that I had received, and giving patience and compassion, I was restored. That presence of the Divine Third had met each of us—giver and recipient—at the point of our individual need, and we each received the bounty of His love.

What happens, though, when a spiritual director takes advantage of those he is directing? How can a seeker avoid manipulative tendencies of those who would seek power over another? Aren't there safeguards to keep an innocent but immature disciple from being exploited, abused, or misled? What about the conflict between trusting one's instincts and trusting another person?

The other side of the coin of difficulty shows up when someone avoids a relationship with a spiritual director out of fear. Some of us will hide our pride and ego behind the fear of being hurt or the fear of being betrayed. "I could never tell anybody *that*" or "Some things are just too personal to share" are common excuses for avoiding the closeness of spiritual direction.

"Shouldn't we just leave well enough alone?" is another way to

169

avoid facing issues from the past that naturally and normally come out in the course of spiritual direction. I am reminded of Florence Littauer's wisdom: "Yes, leave well enough alone . . . if it is well enough."

It has been helpful to me through the years to heed the advice of some ancient sage who counseled that one should never give awe to any other being than God Himself. I think that guideline fits with the teaching of Christ's to "seek first the Kingdom," to place the rule of Christ at the center, and then to move out to others from that center. In other words, it is essential to keep the spiritual director or any human instrument in his rightful place and not put him up on a pedestal for worship.

The relationship between soul friends is a delicate one and must not be taken lightly. There are perils implicit within such a friendship that we must be aware of. But God can be trusted to lead us to the matchups He intends when we offer the process to God.

Within the relationship of soul friends, it is important to remember that, while God may speak through another human being to you, it is ultimately up to you to make decisions and to live your life. It is not fair to expect another human being to come up with your answers. His job is to ask the right questions and to put you in touch with God so that God can speak directly to you.

If you have a gnawing feeling in your stomach or a restlessness in your mind about a relationship in spiritual direction, take that concern to your prayer and meditation time. Ask God what the problem is. Sit in the silence with the picture of the three of you—you, the other person, and Christ—and see what message comes to you. If you persist in prayer, God will show you any unholy alliances. He will also let you know whether your gnawing feeling is a warning about that relationship or simply your fear of being known and being close.

It is wise to stay on the alert within a soul friendship. Going back to sleep will lead to dependency or the transferring of unmet needs onto the other person. Without consciousness, the directee may recreate old patterns of parent/child relationships and stay stuck in nonproductive dynamics.

Recognize that it must be okay to question and doubt within the relationship. It must be okay to say no to anything that violates your integrity, your dignity, or your personhood. Blind obedience within human relationships sets up unhealthy dynamics and abuse. It ultimately leads to disaster. If a spiritual director will not allow you to disagree with him, run for the nearest exit!

Check out your teacher or director. Does his life mesh with what he is teaching you? Does anything he says contradict the teachings of Scripture, or does he use Scripture to justify something about which you feel uncomfortable? Does he set you free to make your own decisions and form your own opinions? Does he honor the fact that God has a personal relationship with you, aside from him, and that God can also speak directly to you? Does he acknowledge that God might also be speaking to him through you?

"Lean on my faith right now," Sandra told me one bitter day when my own faith faltered. "I know you are stumbling, so count on my faith in you and my faith in God."

I was strengthened by the offer, and, indeed, I leaned on her faith more than once. Never, however, has she said, "Think as I think. Do as I do, or do as I say." Nor has she abandoned me when the Spirit of God within me has led me to different conclusions or when I disagreed with a point of view. The freedom Jesus allowed others is an essential ingredient of soul friendship. The truth is that no human being is *always* right.

My trust in Sandra grew as I saw that she walked the walk she talked. She never walks it perfectly, *but neither does she claim to do so!* The point is that when she falls down and gets "off the beam," as she calls it, she gets back up and starts again.

God spoke harsh and severe criticism through prophets of the Old Testament to those priests who required others to observe religious traditions and rituals but neglected those very disciplines themselves. Indeed, the problem with many so-called spiritual leaders is in thinking that the same rules that apply to others do not apply to them.

A spiritual director must do his homework and do it consistently and faithfully. Otherwise, he may slip into that ego-centered state in which he fashions glossy images of what a spiritual leader "should be." Without the humbling process of submission to the teachings of Christ, a spiritual leader may fall into the trap of buying into his "role" in order to live up to the adoration of his students or followers. A teacher or guide must embody the principles he teaches.

Involving oneself in a relationship of spiritual direction does not mean, then, giving up the boundaries of personhood or ceasing to do your own thinking. Surrendering to a teacher or a director never involves surrendering will or integrity. Nor does the relationship mean that you cannot end the relationship. Often the Spirit of Christ quickens one or the other in a relationship, alerting them that it is time to end the regular gatherings of accountability or to change the terms of the relationship. Prayer is a vital key in discerning the movement of the friendship and in giving the courage to move away from each other.

I recall a relationship between an older woman, Blanche, and Diane, who was a new, eager, young Christian. In the first stages of the relationship, there was great joy and delight as the teacher taught the student the ways of prayer and Bible study. Because this student was so willing, the teacher's natural dominating personality began to take over, little by little, in such seemingly insignificant ways that the teacher didn't notice and the student didn't think it mattered.

In this case, Diane entered immediately into an unusually deep and powerful prayer life. For a young Christian, she moved quickly into the depths of knowing Christ, and therefore she was especially sensitive to the leading of God's Spirit. Her prayer life nourished her Bible study and her fellowship with Blanche, and that supportive, loving friendship provided an environment in which Diane flourished.

Within a couple of years, however, Blanche began advising Diane about where she should go and what she should do. When Diane followed another way, Blanche would "punish" Diane by withdrawing from her and not returning her calls, and then by criticizing her, even in the presence of others. When Diane did not buckle under Blanche's criticism, Blanche accused her of not appreciating "all she had done for her."

At first, as Diane prayed, she confessed her own rebellious spirit. She asked God to forgive her for resenting Blanche's interference in her life, and she asked God to give her a willing spirit to receive the direction Blanche gave. The more Diane prayed, however, the more uncomfortable she became with Blanche's domineering spirit. When Diane pictured Christ standing between the two of them, she sensed a darkness like a heavy cloud. Diane recognized the darkness as God's Spirit, leading her to acknowledge the dis-ease between the two of them.

As Diane grew in wisdom and knowledge, her impulsive nature softened and she waited in patience for the right time to move. She continued to offer to God the problem with her spiritual director, praying for the knowledge of God's will within the relationship and for the power to carry out His will. Soon she knew that she must confront Blanche with her feelings. She also knew that the way Blanche received the confrontation would tell Diane what she should do next.

As it turned out, Blanche blew up before Diane could carry out her carefully prayed-out confrontation, and the relationship ended. Diane learned the powerful truth that those who would help others should also be getting help. Those who enter into a relationship in which others are accountable to them would do well to make sure they, too, have that same kind of spiritual accountability with someone else.

Another way to guard against abuse of the spiritual direction relationship is to recognize that the director is not to do for the directee what he must do for himself. That relationship is no substitute for the directee's own hard work of prayer and meditation, Bible study, journaling, worship, service, and giving. The director can only facilitate the journey; the directee must be willing to get his hands dirty in the sin of his own life, and he must also be willing to take responsibility for cleaning up his own act.

When that directee is not willing to do his own work, the director must be willing to confront him. If the director is not willing to speak the truth in love, the director is failing him and enabling him to remain in his comfortable immaturity. A director who tries to do the directee's work for him will wind up in that terrible state of being used, of being forced to admit that "helping you is hurting me."

The true test of a spiritual director is the test of a good parent: Is he or she guiding you and empowering you to live without him? A spiritual director must reflect the heart of a good parent who longs for the child to be able to stand on his own two feet and take care of himself. A spiritual director must be able to rejoice when the directee discovers that the Kingdom of God is within him, and when the directee no longer needs the director, but loves him and wants to share life with him.

"You must get to the point of calling when you need to call instead of putting your needs on hold until they reach crisis proportions," Sandra told me. "Putting yourself in the position of 'bothering me,' at any time of day or night, is part of your growing." She knew that asking for presence, interfering with another's schedule, or "bothering" someone was a big problem for me. She also knew that I did not want to abuse her availability.

"You don't know that sharing this with you helps me out of my own loneliness," she told me one day when I apologized for taking up so much of her time. "I need this, too, Jeanie, to keep me on track."

Never was Sandra unavailable to me when I needed her counsel. Never did she turn me away when I called. Not one time did she say or do anything that made me feel that I was in the way.

Last fall, however, she moved away for a period of time, and I was left on my own. I wondered how I would do without the weekly check-in. Indeed, I have missed her deeply, but the counsel and the love she lavished on me when she was here keeps coming to my remembrance to feed and guide me during this period.

Recently, we met for the first time in months in a new restaurant. Picking up where we had left off, we shared a holy hour, catching up and moving on into the next phase of our lives.

And so, God weaves His love between seekers to bind us together on the perilous journey of wholeness.

12
The Healing Body

If you scorn the fellowship of the brethren, you reject the call of Jesus Christ, and thus your solitude can only be hurtful to you.

—Dietrich Bonhoeffer

Therefore, if anyone is in Christ, he is a new creation; the old has gone, the new has come! All this is from God, who reconciled us to himself through Christ and gave us the ministry of reconciliation.

2 Corinthians 5:17, 18

———✎———

I struck a match to light the first candle of our Advent wreath. It was especially important to me to light that beginning candle this year, for there was a shadow over Christmas for me.

Rumors of war cast a pall on the nation. There was economic bad news, and the stories of banking scandals and drug abuse prevailed among the attempts to spread good news.

If things weren't bad enough in the secular world, there seemed to me to be so much darkness in Christendom this year, and so I wanted to do something to remind myself that hope was still possible. The words of my Jewish friend haunted me throughout the season: "If this is Christianity," she said to me about the offensive behavior of a mutual acquaintance, "count me out."

I can't figure out why it is that we who sponsor the Christmas season can't seem to get along with each other. It just doesn't make sense to me that we who turn the spotlight on Christmas and talk and sing about the Light who came into the darkness can't seem to get out of the darkness of suspicion and confusion. We who are called to model a radical love for each other can't even figure out who the *real* enemy is! We get all entrapped in our expectations and demands of each other and treat each other as the enemy.

Through a lifetime of living in a minister's home and being closely involved with a local body of believers, I have witnessed firsthand the brokenness of the institutional church. I know its imperfections well. My memory holds the wrongs done by Christians to each other. While I rarely think about those painful experiences, there are times when something within our own church family triggers these memories, and the agony of rejection that I felt pierces the present, staining my current feelings about what it means to be the church.

There are other instances, picked up from years of being involved in Christ's body. A particularly vivid memory is of Susan, a young woman from an exceptionally dysfunctional family, who responded to the warmth in our church family as an orphan might respond to the security of a home. Susan brought high expectations to our church. She expected the church to help her financially, and when she and her children came down with the flu, she called upon the members to care for her children while she recuperated. She even asked for clothes for herself and her children.

It didn't take too many weeks for Susan's demanding nature to wear thin. Those who had welcomed her with open arms began to be busy when she called. The very ones who had told her about Christ's love started avoiding her in the halls of the church. Very quickly, Susan became disillusioned because the church didn't meet her expectations. It became a challenge for us who had loved her into the community to walk with her to maturity in her faith.

Susan was a quick learner, however, and she stayed with us through the readjustment of her expectations. She caught on to the reality that the church was not simply a filling station, as some love to call it, but a place of both giving and receiving. Soon, Susan was taking part in giving to others as well as receiving.

"I've found help in my Twelve Step group that I never found in the church," a young man told me. "They accept me as I am and I feel that I really belong there." I have heard that indictment of the church more times than I can count, and it always causes grief. I would love for each church to be a haven of grace and peace for the broken and wounded. I would love for my church to be a place of safety and meaning and purpose for the lost and lonely.

"I'm through with church," another single woman cried bitterly. "I've never felt such censure. I feel condemned when I am there. If I don't agree with the Bible teacher, he thinks I'm not a real Christian!"

We who celebrate Love's Advent into the world often get so hung up on the letter of the law that we break the highest law, the law of love. It makes me think that we haven't learned much from Christmas Past when we break the bonds of love with each other. Nor does it bode well for Christmas Future when we who sponsor the show can't remember who the Director of it really is. We imperfect Christians distort the teachings of Christ and dim the light of Christmas Present by our dysfunctional ways.

As I understand it, the central figure of the Christmas season is the Prince of Peace, Jesus Christ Himself, and I am having a great deal of trouble seeing the consistency between what we *sing* about peace and what we live. We who put on the show of Christmas may very well know the words, but some of us have forgotten the music. We who have been given the Light think that we can decide who gets to bask in the glow of the Light—and who can't.

The breakdown of my own denomination has created irreparable harm in the lives of individuals and in the eyes of the unbelieving world. That dissension is only a reflection, however, of the breakdown of peace among the individual churches. Rare is the church that attempts to take seriously its call to model Christ's life and love.

Recently, our local church leaders made a decision that created some controversy within the membership. There was talk in town about what Southland had done and what others might do in response to that decision.

"How we handle this among ourselves," I heard Martus say over and over, "speaks more loudly than the decision itself."

On the evening of the town meeting that was held as an open forum for the discussion of the issue, many members filled the worship center, and there was electricity in the air. I watched with apprehension. I feared broken relationships and hurt feelings.

What joy it is for me to recall that evening, however, when every person felt free to express his opinion and his concern. What love I feel for those folks who, though they found themselves on opposite sides of the issue, could speak to one another in love and then leave in peace. How splendid it is to see folks taking seriously the respect and honor due each brother and sister in Christ!

That kind of fellowship happens only in an environment of love and acceptance. It is possible only when the presence of Christ is taken seriously, and the true mission of the church is held up as an ideal to pursue.

Perhaps the greatest disservice the modern church does to its flock is to imply that church is a place to be entertained or a place

179

to go with a list of demands. The greatest harm we do to new believers is not to let them in on the secret that salvation is both an event and a process. We must let new converts know that belief in Christ is not about being *rescued*, but *delivered*.

"I like a service to turn me on!" I couldn't believe my ears! We television junkies do like to be entertained. It is so much easier to sit passively in front of the tube, switching channels with a flip of the wrist, when something isn't entertaining enough. That spectator sport is a good deal easier than the real, everyday, flesh-and-blood efforts of participating in a viable Body of Christ, carrying out the mission of Christ.

The church's mission is not to titillate us or to lull us into a false state of euphoria. The mission of the church is to empower each of us to become instruments of God's love and grace in the world, and then to send us out into the marketplaces we inhabit as salt and light in a dark and empty world. I have learned that, in being an instrument of healing, I become healed.

Last year, when the parable of the Good Samaritan kept creeping into my prayer time, I began to see in new ways that it is not the legalism or the professionalism of religion that will cure the woundedness of any of us. Indeed, it was the outcast who performed the act of mercy in the story, and it is often the outcast of society whom Christ uses to bring healing to others.

"I have finally found some answers," a young seeker told me, "but you wouldn't find my helpers in your church. You wouldn't let one of them teach the kids, and they probably couldn't be deacons, but they have shown me Christ's love as I have never seen it before."

I squirmed under what I was hearing. What is it about the typical church that so often keeps people from getting the help they need? And why is it that those who find it elsewhere become angry with the church for not giving it to them?

"Why do we stay in it?" Martus and I ask each other now and

then, when the going gets tough. Both of us grew up in ministers' homes, and so the church has been a part of our lives, like a family member, all of our lives. However, the truth is that both of us love both the idea of the church and the living out of the dailiness of Christ's Body. We believe in it. And we believe that God has called us to work within it at this time.

It is, then, my attachment to the church that makes its imperfections so painful. The brokenness in Christendom creates jagged edges in my heart, and the brokenness among us casts a loathsome shadow on the season for me. These growing edges cut and burn, and not one of us can escape the consequences of our plight.

I yearn for harmony and unity to flow within the rich diversity. I long for the time when we can major in what is most important, letting the Christmas spirit flow unhindered by our fears and suspicions of each other. Indeed, my Christmas prayer is an ongoing prayer for a true peace for all of us. I keep asking myself and any of my sisters and brothers in Christ who will stop long enough, when will we lay down egotism and be willing to share the splendor of Christ's love and grace and peace. When will we be willing to take personal responsibility for being a conduit of that splendor in the world?

Again, I return to the reality that I am responsible for my own churchmanship. For this season of my life, I am accountable to my church family for my own stewardship of the blessings of God. I am called to be the best instrument I can be within the body of believers called Southland Baptist Church.

I am fortunate to be in the particular church I am in, for its body life gave me courage and strength and hope to continue lighting my Advent candle throughout the days of December. My candle and my church keep reminding me of the Light that illuminates the darkest night. It keeps me remembering the Love that conquers the deepest hate. My candle of hope soothes those jagged edges of fear and despair, turning my heart and attention to the Source of Peace, and giving me strength to keep on keeping on spreading the splendor of Christmas.

There is another, more intimate (and yes, more risky) way to experience the shared splendor of life together, and that is within the challenge of a spiritual growth group. In a powerful way, the growth groups of my experience become "church," that is, a body of believers committed to the shared life of Christ-between.

A spiritual growth group is a unique group process. It is not a Bible study group, although it must be based on biblical principles. In the spiritual growth groups that I lead, Scripture is intermingled with other materials; participants are encouraged to make regular Bible study a central focus of their own spiritual disciplines. I have discovered that, while I encourage and promote daily Bible study, each individual adapts his study to his own pace.

A spiritual growth group is not a prayer group, although prayer is a vital link in the entire process. Members are encouraged to make prayer and meditation part of their daily discipline. They are also encouraged to pray for one another. Periodically, in the group, when one of the members has shared a need, I will remind the group that they now know better how to pray for that person.

And, in a way, being in the group is, in itself, prayer. Being open to each other and to God while the group is in process is a way to practice the presence of God. Now and then, I remind the group that God is present, that He is part of the dynamics of the group process, and that that is prayer.

Howard Hovde, the director of Laity Lodge and a special friend, tells one of my favorite stories about "praying with your eyes open." Howard tells of an appointment he had with a priest when he was seeking spiritual direction. The two men spent a few

182

moments talking about the terms of the spiritual direction, and then Howard said, "Could we pray together?"

The priest paused for a moment, and then he said, "I thought that was what we were doing."

Spiritual growth groups are not therapy groups or encounter groups. They are not solely about self-discovery, although that takes place. They are not simply psychological exercises, although it is important that sound psychological principles undergird the processes. Spiritual growth groups place primary importance on God's presence in and among and through the group process. They are for discovering where God is at work and for hearing what God is saying to a particular life circumstance. Spiritual growth groups act in God's stead in loving the individual, and *in that process*, therapy takes place.

In the growth groups that I lead, I must emphasize the fact that the spirituality is *Christian* spirituality. It is my intentional choice to teach and write out of a belief in the centrality of Christ, and the ultimate goal of whatever I do is to lead others to a personal, vital love relationship with Jesus Christ.

Through the years, as I have facilitated groups that focus on personal, spiritual growth, there have been weeks of plugging along when it seemed that nothing was "happening." The same thing can happen in one's prayer life: There are periods of dryness and times of going through the motions.

Sometimes the group members are open with one another and sometimes they aren't. Each group experience, and each collection of seekers, is different. Taking the awareness of Christ into the group process keeps me open to what is going on in and among us.

"I hate these stupid sheets you give us," one of my longtime group members tells me. For each group, I prepare sheets of discussion-starters, and I give them "growthwork" (a better term than homework!) to use in quiet time between groups. My Big

Resister complains a lot, but she always does her growthwork, and she has kept coming back for six years.

"I need the group's support," she says. "And I grow when I put myself in the position of challenging old ways."

"Besides," another added, "when I don't stay in a group of accountability, I forget what I have learned. I need you to remind me of what I so easily forget."

I savor those moments when group members spontaneously acknowledge and celebrate the value of the spiritual growth group process. Those moments are rare, and they cannot be programmed, any more than Christ's Voice can be programmed, manipulated, or contrived. The moments of "knowing" are sacred, and they are gifts.

"My worship is so much more meaningful to me when I stay in this group," one of the ladies told a group recently. "It is as if I take care of my confessional needs here, so that when I attend the worship service, I can focus on praising God."

"This group has become my family," said another. "It is like all of you are my mother." This group member, like many, had an aching gap in her experience of motherlove. Therefore, she had a problem letting down her guard with "a bunch of females." She said she had always preferred the company of men.

"I know what you mean," added her best friend, "except it feels more like sisters to me." This participant didn't have the negative mother-images that her friend had, but she did know the joy of the sisterhood, gathered around the Growth Options group room once a week. "I had never really known other women except in a competitive way in my work," she continued. "It feels so good to have a safe place where I can explore my feelings and experiences without fear of being ridiculed and with the trust that what I say will stay here."

While the most recent groups I have led have been with women, Martus and I have led numerous Yokefellow Spiritual

Growth Groups together. Both of us believe that the small support group is one of the most valuable ways of sharing the love of Christ and living out the Kingdom of God.

One night, in a Marriage Enrichment Support Group that met once a week for many months, the tender presence of love was almost tangible. We had explored the selfishness that marriage evokes in the partners. Some had looked at the ways their selfishness governed their use or misuse of time or money. Others dealt with the fear of being open in communication, which is a form of selfishness and self-protection.

We had begun the group meeting with a guided meditation in which we asked the group members to lay down the cares and worries of the day and be present to whatever gift of grace Christ had for them that Monday night. Because of the personal spiritual devotion of the members of that particular group, it was easy for the awareness of the presence of Christ, as Teacher, Leader, Healer, and Guide, to be experienced.

As we worked with our individual issues, there was an unusual amount of understanding between couples and between partners. There seemed to be an unusual number of times when a much-needed awareness or insight would break through an impasse. On occasion, there were tears as the spirit of forgiveness was released and partners moved from binding each other to an old hurt to setting each other free.

In a deep, spiritual sense, we were washing each other's feet that night in the safe haven of our church den. By our listening to each other and by our quiet presence with each other, we were serving each other the bread and wine of Christ's love. Giving support, hearing each other in love, and affirming each other's value and giftedness paved the way for an occasion of grace, and we left knowing that we had been on holy ground.

Sharing this love of Christ, whether in a spiritual growth group or a church body, has its natural pitfalls *that are necessary for its growth and maturity.* Those problems with a group of believers are necessary if the church is going to become what God intends it to become. The problems are opportunities to know God better.

Because any group operates like a family system and is composed of broken, needy, self-centered individuals, the church, regardless of its size, contains within itself the potentiality of becoming dysfunctional. One member's brokenness affects the whole, and one member's growth toward wholeness influences everyone's growth. Part of the meaning, then, of the irritations and agonies within the body lies in God's desire to deliver each member from his own oppression, and sometimes He uses the church or the group to bring that about.

What is this submission stuff about? I thought to myself while teaching some of the letters of Paul one year. *And how do we live that out today? Will it really work, or will the more dominant individuals run over those who are more compliant and adaptive?*

As I continued in my journey of discovery through prayer, I began to recognize opportunities for learning on the job about submission. To be honest, I bucked at the way the first lessons came, for they came through pain and confrontation. The beginning course in submission came because I was the preacher's wife.

"Don't pay any attention to her," a counselor friend told me when I shared a concern about an unusually critical church member. It was the first year of our church's life, and I had run into a person who seemed committed to irritating me. "Write her off," was the advice.

I knew that writing people off and walking away were common ways of dealing with misunderstandings within any church. Folks don't like to make waves or cause trouble, and so sometimes, instead of disagreeing openly, they will simply fade away.

I left the conversation with a troubled heart. I would like to say

that the reason my heart was troubled was that I had such compassion for the troublemaker that I couldn't bear to just "write her
off." The truth of the matter was that my heart was heavy because
I knew that, because of my husband's position, I didn't have a
choice about writing her off or walking away.

Was I ever trapped! Not only did I lack the freedom to do as I
pleased, but I was going to have to deal with my feelings and my
actions and thoughts because the troublemaker would not! It was
up to me to get along. The ball was in my court to figure out how
to make peace with the peace-breaker. My lot in life was to suffer
and not speak, to take it and not give it back.

Fortunately, my spiritual director stepped in. She kept urging
me to take my gaze off the problem and turn it toward God. I
knew that was what I needed to do, but what I was doing was
entirely different. I would gaze at that problem, turning scenarios
and conversations with her over and over in my mind. I would
look for the things she did to irritate me and then make sure I
reported them to Martus at the first available opportunity.

Sandra kept after me, however, urging me to look inside myself to see what this person was evoking in me. She guided me to
see how I was projecting my own hidden, but powerful, faults
onto the other person. And then she asked me to see that person
through the eyes of God's love. That was the last straw!

Through the process of healing the brokenness in my own life,
as it was being lived out in my resentment toward this troublemaker, I learned an invaluable lesson. The best thing about
being a minister's wife is that I cannot run away. I have to learn
to get along, and that is a gift of grace and mercy. My unwritten
job description contains an unexpected word: love.

In learning to tolerate, accept, and love others within the
body, I have learned to tolerate and accept myself. In forgiving
the ones I least understand, I have come to accept forgiveness for
those parts of myself. In giving respect and honor to others who

come from different histories and have different needs from mine, I have learned what it is to *submit* to others with the Body.

In struggling to knead my mind to understand another's viewpoint, which is different from mine, I have come to know more clearly what I believe and what I don't believe. In expressing my own viewpoints and yearnings to people who don't necessarily understand or agree with me, but are willing to allow my differentness, I have learned about God's amazing grace.

When I forget that the Living Christ is at work among His children, I recall the words of George MacDonald:

> The Lord Jesus, by free, potent communion with their inmost being, will change His obedient brethren till in every thought and impulse they are good like Him, unselfish, neighborly, brotherly like Him, loving the Father perfectly like Him, ready to die for the truth like Him, caring for Him for nothing in the universe but the will of God, which is love, harmony, liberty, beauty, and joy.

God uses some powerful models within our church family to reveal His faithfulness and compassion. Those who give freely of their time, energy, and money to perpetuate the work of the Kingdom through this local church have shown me in living color what service means. They have accepted me and helped me to love myself.

Members of spiritual growth groups have forgiven me when I have failed, picked me up when I was down, and encouraged me to go forward in becoming the person God intended me to be. Through the power that is set loose among us when we come together, I have learned what it is to be loved with Christ's love.

Indeed, sharing life within the body of Christ involves a getting mixed up with each other's lives, just as God, through the Incarnation, got all mixed up with the seamiest sides of human life on earth.

Incarnating Christ to each other involves a sharing of the deaths and the births. We tremble corporately at the death of each marriage. We are scarred by the wounds of each other's addictions. Our corporate faith and hope are stained by the imperfections we bring together, but in keeping our focus on Christ, somehow we limp along toward wholeness. And every so often, one of us bounds into the wider places of God's grace in an amazing leap of spiritual growth.

My favorite service at our church is the Christmas Eve Service. On that evening, the chairs in our worship center are arranged in the round, with the Advent candles on a round table in the center.

By the time the girls and I make it to the late service, I have flour under my nails and in my hair from the day's baking and cooking. We rush around to arrive in plenty of time to sit at our traditional place; it isn't often we get to sit as a family in worship. Once seated, I breathe a huge sigh of relief. The bulk of the work of celebrating is done and I can relax in the beauty of the celebration.

I like to get there early and watch the crowd gather in the candlelit sanctuary. Seated in a circle, there is an intimacy, even though the sanctuary is packed with people. Waiting for the service to begin, we savor the Christmas music and look around the room, smiling our blessing to each other.

I see the beloved faces of college students who have returned home for the holidays. Here and there are families who are missing a member this year; other families have added a member. I note the children who weren't big enough to come last year, but who now take their places with the family—the church family and the nuclear family.

This past year, my friend Jack Goss was missing. I closed my eyes at the piercing memory of Jack's faithful stance by the back door. Jack "stood guard," almost, from the church's inception, watching to see who needed help, making sure those who were homebound had a visit, picking up cans to sell at the recycling center to help pay for the building of the body of believers he loved.

Jack Goss pretended to be tough and gruff, but it was he who delivered meals to the elderly, and it was he who stayed in the kitchen until every dish was washed at the New Members' Dinners. It was Jack who gave his business experience to the Baptist Children's Home in Beeville. And it was Jack who pastored Martus and me, quietly standing by and giving acceptance and forgiveness and support through the arduous years of building a brand new church family.

In the quietness of Christmas Eve, I recalled the moments after the memorial service for Jack. After the family meal, I stood in the door of the kitchen, watching a former mayor and a retired bank president washing dishes out of love for their friend, Jack, and living out their own servanthood.

These were strong, capable, influential people in the kitchen that new spring day. Jack's friends are independent West Texans, accustomed to positions of power and responsibility. On that day, however, all of us felt a keen sense of neediness. We kept hugging each other that day, asking over and over, "How do people who don't have a church family make it through times like this?"

There is a tenderness among my church family that pervades the meetings and fellowships and ministries. There is a tenderness about our Christmas Eve Service that has an almost tangible, luminous glow about it. I know that the splendor of that one night doesn't have anything to do with how the chairs are arranged or how pretty the Christmas dresses are. That splendor of Christmas Eve is the result of what goes on the rest of the year among this body of believers. The glow around us on Christmas Eve is the shared splendor of Christ's presence among us. It is as if Christ grants us an extra sense of His presence. Perhaps He is saying to us, wounded and faulty as we are, "You are my beloved children, and in you I am well pleased."

At the conclusion of the Christmas Eve Service, Martus lights the candles of the servers from the light of the Christ candle. I almost hold my breath, like an expectant child as, one by one, each of us receives light from his neighbor and then, in turn, passes it to the next person. Year after year, I anticipate that moment when the candlelight grows and grows, one by one, until the darkened sanctuary is filled with light.

I stand with my brothers and sisters in Christ, my children, my friends, my husband, with whom I have lived and loved, laughed, and learned. I rise to my feet to sing "Joy to the World, the Lord is come!" with these fellow pilgrims with whom I rejoice and agonize and slog through the muck and the glory of daily living, and I know that we share a precious treasure, the splendor of the Living Christ.

It is that sharing of Christ's presence that empowers me to carry the light out into each new year.

13
Here . . . and Beyond

I could not help wondering why it is that those who *seek*
after the Truth find themselves in essential harmony, even
unity, with other seekers; but those who *have* the Truth
seem to have a bottomless enmity for those who do not have
it, or have another truth.

—James P. Carse

Blessed are the peacemakers, for they will be called sons of
God.

Matthew 5:9

"Let there be peace on earth, and let it begin with me. . . ."
My family and I made our way to our car from the Glenn
Junior High School choir program, filled with goodwill and hol-
iday cookies, singing together the signature song of peace that
ends every Glenn concert.

"Merry Christmas!" we called to other families, and they to us.
What a great way to begin the Christmas season! How good it is
to live in a community like ours! Who minded the cold weather
when there was such warmth in human hearts! I sighed with
contentment and called the family's attention to brilliant stars
twinkling peacefully in the clear West Texas sky.

Even as we piled into our car, however, the peace of the
moment was shattered by a vicious argument over who had called

"shotgun," the front passenger seat. Once the peaceful spell was broken, arguments and squabbles broke out like chicken pox, grating my ears and grinding my nerves, so recently soothed by music and friendship.

"Let there be peace on earth," I began to sing, more out of a motivation to shame my warring clan than to bring peace.

"And let it begin with *you*," one of the girls chimed in, and the whole family burst into laughter.

How typical it is to look to someone else to take the first step to making peace! How common it is for each of us to think that if only *they* would change or quit doing what they are doing, peace would come.

Continuing the drive home, our calm restored with laughter, I thought of the severest lie of the Evil One: the idea that there can be extended or permanent peace. What happened in my family happens globally. Peace is a fragile gift that must be guarded and perpetuated *intentionally*, and each of us is responsible for making peace where we are.

Perhaps the reason that world peace is so shaky and elusive is that individual and family peace is so difficult to achieve. Perhaps the reason I want others—my husband, my leaders, the president—to make peace is that I feel so overwhelmed with the challenge of creating peace within my own life.

Is it possible that the area of human relationships is the greatest "mission field" of Christians today? Is it possible that "passing the peace," creating harmony at home and with each other, is the most piercing call for those of us who claim the name of the Prince of Peace?

Does what I do as an individual to create peace within my own sphere ripple out to the larger sphere? Can I, one solitary life, make any kind of difference?

The news stories of people gathering around the world to meditate about world peace flickered through my mind. "Harmonic convergence" was a new term I little understood. I was hearing more and more stories about people outside traditional denominational lines who were praying for peace. Was the secular world filling a need that the church has not met?

Last fall, I stood before nine hundred college students from fourteen different college campuses in Texas. It was my task to lead them through several periods of extended silence and prayer. Looking out over the crowd, I took a few deep breaths. How would Aggies take to silence? And what about those sophisticated students from the University of Texas? Most of all, I was concerned about how my daughter, a freshman at Baylor, would receive her mother's guidance. I prayed I wouldn't embarrass her in front of her new friends. This was, I thought, the acid test: Would practicing the presence of Christ in creative silence speak to the coming generation?

The day before, I listened to a tape recording someone had sent me. The speaker, in describing the readiness of individuals for the deeper life, stated that today's young people are seeking a deeper spirituality earlier *because the world has done such violence to them.*

I recalled that speech, looking out at the tender faces lifted in my direction. I set the stage for their hours of silence and then asked them to leave the huge tabernacle without speaking to each other. To my utter amazement, there was hardly a sound as those young pilgrims made their way outside, finding seclusion under trees and on the grassy knolls of the encampment grounds.

I wept at their openness to the possibility that God would meet them in the silence of the morning. My heart broke at their availability and reverence. And I gave thanks that they were beginning a spiritual journey at such a tender age.

On one of the last stops of my trip to Europe, we took a two-hour tour of the cathedral in Cologne, Germany. The cathedral had only recently been fully restored from the bombings of World War II. Weary of tours and crowds by now, and yearning for the solitude that has become essential to my day, I slipped away from the group and made my way to one of the prayer chapels.

Gratefully, I crept into the cool comfort of this dim chapel. As has become my custom when visiting a chapel or cathedral with kneeling benches, I pulled down the bench and knelt for prayer, moving instinctively into the familiar words of the Prayer of Abandonment:

> *Father,*
> *I abandon myself into Your hands;*
> *do with me what You will.*
> *Whatever You may do, I thank You:*
> *I am ready for all,*
> *I accept all.*
> *Let only Your will be done in me,*
> *and in all Your creatures—*
> *I wish no more than this, O Lord.*
>
> *Into Your hands I commend my soul;*
> *I offer it to You with all the love of my heart*
> *for I love You, Lord,*
> *and so need to give myself,*
> *to surrender myself into Your hands,*
> *without reserve,*
> *and with boundless confidence,*
> *For You are my Father.*
>
> > *Charles de Foucauld's*
> > *personalized translation of*
> > *The Lord's Prayer*

After a few moments of my own interior silence, I was keenly aware both of the presence of Christ and of the presence of others coming and going in the small room. Quietly, I eased myself back onto the wooden pew and opened my eyes. Ancient stone walls and stained-glass windows sheltered the pray-ers, most of whom were very young or very old.

My eyes wandered from face to face. Even as I observed these present supplicants, I tried to imagine the thousands of people who, for centuries, had made their way here, for thousands of reasons, to bow in prayer. My imagination stretched to picture how it must have been to have prayed in this room during the wars.

Suddenly, I felt that unity of Christ's Spirit that comes as a rare gift. Here, thousands of miles from my home and my own church, I felt "at-one-ment" with those whose language I could not speak nor understand. In this foreign land, I was at home, surrounded by others who believed that prayer would make a difference in the way life went.

That splendid moment remains a souvenir, far more precious to me than any I could have bought. Sharing that powerful presence with strangers engraved itself on my heart much more than seeing the relics of the Three Magi encased in gold.

Within a week of my return home, I joined a group of community leaders. The small talk before lunch centered on the opening of the Berlin Wall and the thawing of the Cold War. We marveled about what was happening in Russia—our country's greatest enemy was now becoming our ally. Peace had a chance at last, we agreed.

Later, as we ate, we discussed ways to solve some of the problems in our community. I listened, quietly at first, as the others discussed some of the difficulties. Strangely, I kept recalling those television images of people streaming through the openings of the Berlin Wall. I kept seeing the Germans with whom I had worshiped only last week. The sights and sounds of that restored sanctuary kept bubbling up in my memory, even as we talked about the warring spirits in our community.

Listening to the wielders of power in my hometown, I thought of Scott Peck's wisdom in his book on community building, *The Different Drum*. "Community neither comes naturally nor is it purchased cheaply," he said. *How true*, I thought. And the more I listened to the conversation at our table, the more I wondered what I was doing at this luncheon.

"We've got to figure out how to deal with those egos," one leader at our table remarked, and we all knew that he was referring to the adversaries of harmony and progress in our community.

"I think the place to begin is with my own ego," I replied, only to wait in silence as the others at the table looked down at their plates. I had warned them that I had simple suggestions and jet lag!

"All I have to do to confront my ego," I continued, taking a deep, deep breath, "is to walk into the door of my home, where I discover my incredible need to control." And then I bit my tongue. The sorry truth was that I wanted to control this group, too, by convincing them that their egos were as big as those of their "adversaries."

Indeed, it is ego that makes us humans define an enemy. It is ego that causes us children masquerading as adults to choose up sides, to pit "us" against "them," to create separations among us. When we are under the control of self-will or of ego, we can't accept God's help and we can't see things the way they really are. *What happens at the global level is but a reflection of what happens at the dinner tables around the world.*

Ego takes over in community life just as it takes over at the family dinner table. Just as individuals must deal with ego and with evil if there is to be peace, so must communities. The problem comes when we think that we can deal with corporate evil without confronting that which is in the individual heart. As Thomas Merton says, "The temptation is, then, to account for my fault by seeing an equivalent amount of evil in someone else."

What would it take, I wondered later, to get us human beings to lay down that need to control or the tendency to be controlled and to begin to act like free agents, responsible and loving, and willing to give up our own self-will in order for the will of God to be released? What would it take for us to learn how to submit to each other? Doesn't our survival itself depend on our learning how to get along?

More personally, I had to take a long, hard look at what I, one solitary woman, could possibly do to facilitate love and peace within my community. Preparing for my speech to community leaders forced me to call myself into account for the quality of my own witness to the Light of Christ. Frankly, I came up short in peacemaking, but long on desire to make a difference by the way I live my life and through the words I speak and write.

A greater test was to come. Within less than six months of this luncheon, war broke out in the Persian Gulf. In less than a year after the thawing of Eastern Europe and Russia, a new enemy, Saddam Hussein, emerged, to take the place of last year's enemy. What I had believed was unthinkable was now being played out.

Amy, my youngest daughter, counted down the days to the United Nations' deadline of January 15. This was to be the day Hussein must withdraw from Kuwait. Each morning, at the breakfast table, Amy would say, "Only six more days until we know if we are going to war."

"Do you think there will be war, Mom?" she would ask each morning, and I would look into her somber brown eyes and assure her that I didn't really think so. "Surely," I would say with sincere confidence, "they will find a way through this."

Amy is thirteen, long and lovely. She swings her shiny hair over her shoulder with that carefree grace of girlhood. She and her sisters also bring home wonderful young boys, and in their youth, filled with promise and hope, lies our future. Suddenly, I was looking at them with new eyes.

As the days drew nearer to the deadline, I held out for a peaceful resolution. I refused to join my neighbors in tying yellow ribbons 'round my oak trees. Call it denial if you will, but my mind could not hold the thought that there would be war. In a crazy kind of magical thinking, I must have believed that if I didn't participate in the ribbon rituals, I could stave off war.

I kept on writing this book about Christ's presence in the world, calling up in my memory the teachings of Christ, and then I would go home to watch the news. In utter amazement, I heard other Christians, presumably fellow-heirs with the Prince of Peace, demanding that we "wipe Hussein off the face of the earth," and I shuddered to myself.

Violence *never* ultimately stops violence, either in a family or on the globe. Every violent act ultimately evokes an in-kind reaction. How on earth can calls for war come from the same mouths as "Blessed are the peacemakers"?

I sat in my Sunday school class and listened to powerful and educated citizens grapple with the topics of war and peace, sanctity of life and the violence within, only to be confronted with the agony of being unable to make clean, clear platitudes in the face of impending doom. I heard us, long-accustomed to perceiving our nation as "God's country," long for the simple mind-set that we are right and "they" (whoever the current enemy is) are wrong. I heard sincere Christians justify war as a way of peace.

I watched news accounts of the flooding of people into cathedrals and churches during the days before January 15. Accounts of converts among the forces in Saudi Arabia floated back to the states. Could it be, I wondered, that this deepening darkness of war has done what the ten preceding years of political efforts on the part of religious people have not been able to do?

Is it possible that war has brought people back to a dependence on God when all the efforts to force legislation could not? With astonishment, I watched every single one of the forty-eight time slots on our church's prayer vigil board fill up. These Baptists, always eager for action, came through around the clock in prayer.

Leaving my own appointed time in our prayer vigil, I walked out into the darkness of a brand-new year and wondered again if peace and love and incarnational Christianity were all just a pipe dream. Was I idealistic and simple-minded enough to believe that *one person's* efforts at making peace would make a difference? Was I wrong to think that we Christians, yielded to practicing the presence of Christ and living out the Sermon on the Mount, could change the world?

During the agonizing days of January, I taught the story of the Exodus for the Community Bible Study. Week after week, I delved into the story of Moses and the Pharaoh, and I had to come to terms with the ways we repeat history over and over. I made anguished attempts to understand the insidious way bondage to anything holds both tyrant and victim in a deathgrip. I grappled with the difficulty of defining who is the victim and who really is the tyrant. I recalled Thomas Merton's words that "at the root of all war is fear," and I prayed for healing for all of us.

Through those days of waiting, I called my sister, Kathleen, and made noble, but feeble, efforts to reassure her. Her son Stephen had gone off to war, bringing back the horror of her husband's days in Vietnam. I heard the dread in Kathleen's and John's voices, but I refused to believe that war would come.

I watched the eyes of the young ones around me darken in the past weeks. I heard their horror and fear. I watched them try to process a world-gone-awry that we, their elders, have made for them. I wept in horror and grief that, for whatever reasons, we were allowing war.

On January 16, 1991, I walked in the front door two hours after the bombing of Baghdad had begun. Amy and Julie, trying to study for mid-year finals, were sprawled in front of the television in horror. The three of us huddled together, taking strength and solace from the presence of each other, processing the information that flooded our peaceful family room.

"It's important to establish early who is in control of the sky," boomed an authoritative voice.

"Control of the sky?" Julie gasped, incredulous. "Control of the sky? That's the problem! Don't they know that *God* controls the sky?"

My child, innocent of the ways of military strategy, nevertheless understands a deeper truth, that we get in serious trouble when we get mixed up about who really is in charge of the sky. Forgetting the sovereignty of God is the thing that always breaks the peace, for an individual, a family, a nation, a world.

On January 16, 1991, everything changed. Never again would my children be innocent of war. Never again would the world be the safe playground they had known from birth. Never again would they be ignorant of the ways in which corporate and national evil filters down to the individual. But would they, I wondered, learn that it is individual evil that builds and builds until it erupts into the madness of banking scandals and drug abuse and rape and murder and, ultimately, war.

The next evening, I arrived at Laity Lodge for a Writers' Workshop, led by Madeleine L'Engle. The talk at the dinner table was war. The mood was tense and anxious. How could we be creative with the world falling apart? Wasn't it, somehow, self-indulgent to enjoy this special place when others were suffering? How could we produce anything, even there in those holy spaces of the Frio Canyon?

At first, we thought we would "drop out" for a few days, ignoring the news and concentrating on our assignments. Madeleine, however, suggested that we appoint a "news correspondent" who would gather the news twice a day and deliver it to us at ap-

201

pointed times so that we would remain informed. For the rest of the time, we would leave the world in God's hands and go on about our various assignments.

A special mood emerged out of that workshop. A deeper tenderness, born out of a fresher and keener awareness of the fragile nature of life, washed over us, and the sense of God's loving presence broke out of our fear-torn minds and hearts in creative and powerful expressions of hope and faith and courage.

There, in a world turned upside down, a group of people who believed in the reality of the presence of Christ kept on expressing love, even in the midst of desperation. There, in spite of news accounts, people chose life over death, light over darkness, and love over fear. In that one winter canyon in the Hill Country of Texas, individuals made a deliberate choice to express the hope that was within them, born out of a love-relationship with Jesus Christ.

"We must have courage," our wise teacher kept telling us, "and we must express courage to others."

"Love is the only answer," Madeleine said, "and every act of love ripples out and out and out, with effects that we will never see or know."

Can one solitary individual's prayer life affect the life of the whole? Can practicing the presence of Christ make a difference in these days of horror? What are we, as Christians, as carriers of the Light, to do? What difference does lighting one lone candle in the darkness make?

I came home from the weekend's experience somehow strengthened for the coming days. I came home to ever-increasing warfare, but I came home more determined than ever to persevere in my belief and actions that extending Christ's presence is the very best thing of all that I can do.

"What can we do? What can we do?" people ask around me. "How do we pray?"

There is much to do, and the beginning point in all times of trauma is prayer. We pray for peace, of course, but we pray for peace the same way we pray for healing (and perhaps those are one and the same), leaving the ways and means up to God. We pray constantly and fervently.

Peace activists march across my television screen night after night, shaking their fists at the camera, or standing immobile, holding signs that speak their minds. The protesters have their place, but I want to scream that their effort would be better served by going home and making peace with their loved ones.

We who call ourselves by Christ's name must go into our homes and workplaces and institutions here in the deserts and wastelands of America and act in peace.

Practicing the presence is no longer a luxury. Prayer and meditation are no longer options for those of us whose lives have been changed by the liberating presence of the Living Christ. We carry a divine imperative to go into the world with the message of Christ's love and grace. Now, more than ever before in my lifetime, the world is starving to death for good news and for hope. Christians must be willing to extend that message and share the splendor.

In a newspaper article on dealing with the stress of war, a psychologist listed prayer and meditation as one of the ways of making it through the darkness. "Let God tell you that God is doing the best God can." It was a pointed reminder that even God is working within the restrictions of human will.

Given the reality of the free will, I recognize the importance of aligning my will with God's will, and I acknowledge that sometimes God is doing the best that God can do with me. Now, of

203

all times, we must act out the transforming power of Christ's presence rather than conforming to the world's standards.

When the world says "hoard," we can give. Where the world practices vengeance, we can try forgiving our enemies. Where the world says, "Look out for Number One," we are called to love one another, giving ourselves away. And when the world, mesmerized by endless viewings of the same war scenes over and over and over again, calls us to be afraid, we can express love and hope.

We are to pray for our enemies, and we are to confess the enemy within.

We are to pray for justice, and we are to confess the injustice and meanspirited within.

We are to pray for liberation for all of God's creation, and we are to confess the ways in which we hold others in bondage and the ways in which we remain in bondage.

We are to ask God for peace . . . and then be willing to be His instrument, malleable in His hands, obedient to His guidance.

And we are to pray for love for all. We are to live in love. We are to be Christ's love to each other, holding up the Light of hope day after day.

I cannot speak for any other, but I know that I am called to practice Christ's presence in the midst of my sphere. Part of my challenge lies in reassuring the young that God is ultimately in charge of this planet and of our lives, and part of my responsibility is in keeping on with life-affirming ways that speak Christ's everlasting love.

This week, I retrieved the Christ candle from the Advent wreath that has graced our December table for all the years of our children's lives. At the first evening meal when it was back on the dining table, Julie and Amy wanted to know why the Christ candle was out.

"We will light this Christ candle every evening as a reminder to us to pray for peace," I told them solemnly. "It is to remind us to pray for Stephen and for Kathleen and John and for all the others whose families are touched by war."

"What if the war lasts so long that it burns down," one of my practical children asked.

"Then we will get another candle, and another one after that, if we must," I answered. "We will light this candle as a reminder to ourselves that we are to carry the Light and Love of Christ wherever we go."

Perhaps we will keep a Christ candle always on our dining table, even after war is over, to help us remember the sacred responsibility and privilege of carrying the splendor of Christ's presence.

May Christ's presence fill our lives with peace . . . and may that presence and its splendor illumine our darkened world with peace and hope.

Guidelines for Exercises for Relational Prayer

"Be transformed by the renewing of your mind."

Romans 12:2

⎯⎯⎯∽⎯⎯⎯

The exercises that follow are useful in developing the ability to imagine Christ's presence with you. They are helpful in establishing new thought patterns and in developing the mind of Christ.

In some ways, this process might be compared to installing software in a computer. It is a practical way to choose the pictures and images that play in your head rather than letting habitual, and often negative and self-defeating, pictures control your thoughts.

Imagination is a wonderful gift from God. God uses the faculty of imagination to help us visualize plans and projects and ways to carry them out. He also uses the ability to make mental pictures as a way of helping us help ourselves to solve problems.

There is another, dark side to imagination, however. Sometimes, my mind so easily turns to worry, which is nothing more than picturing, or visualizing, bad things happening, and worry is an insidious, destructive habit. In my experience, I can easily drift into using my imagination to replay scenes in which I was injured or had my feelings hurt or when I made mistakes; the process is almost like playing negative videotapes in my head. Sometimes, too, I use my imagination to create or visualize pictures of what I expect from events or people, thereby setting myself up for disappointment.

It is possible to form new habits of thought, however, and it is possible to take charge of the images that I carry in my head. When I train my mind to practice the presence of Christ, allowing His Spirit to transform my God-given imagination, I change my thoughts and my perspective. As a natural consequence, the feelings and behavior then change, as well. Often, as a result of Christ's transforming presence in my thought patterns, my feelings, and my behavior, there are physiological changes, as well.

As you decide to develop the discipline of practicing the presence of Christ, it is helpful to select a consistent time of day and a regular place for your meditation time. This holy space needs to be a private one, where you can be assured of not being disturbed. It is important to guard this time carefully, giving it first priority without becoming legalistic. Practiced consistently, the meditation time will become as natural in your daily routine as taking care of your physical needs, such as eating and sleeping. Finally, you will come to the place of feeling incomplete without that daily time of prayer and meditation.

Take your journal with you to this appointment with God. Include your Bible or a devotional book. However, since the intent of this time is *listening* and practicing the presence of Christ, you will want to give the bulk of the time to the actual practice of silence.

Some find it helpful to record the following exercises on an audio tape. Others like to play quiet music as a background. It is important that you learn to make friends with silence, however, choosing not to run into the familiar comfort of noise.

As you continue your consistent and deliberate times of solitude, you will discover that those moments of making conscious contact with God will come to you during the day. You will discover that you can carry your inner sanctuary with you wherever you go, and you can practice the presence of Christ in the busiest marketplace.

When you first draw apart, it is helpful to take some time to breathe deeply. Take a few moments to let go of the cares of the day. Remind yourself that you are there to listen and receive. You may want to read Scripture first. However you structure your time with God, expect Him to meet you, and then welcome His coming.

As you become more comfortable with practicing the presence of Christ, you will naturally take the conscious awareness of Him with you as you go about your way. Thus, you will find the meaning to Paul's instruction to "pray without ceasing."

Before beginning this venture in relational prayer, take some time to ponder Matthew 15:19, Proverbs 23:7, and Mark 7:14–23. Another important passage for understanding the intimacy and unity between the Living Christ and our own lives is John 15.

You might want to consult my book on meditation and creativity, *Creative Silence*, for more exercises that help in developing the ability to practice the presence of Christ.

The Scripture given at the end of each meditation is for further meditation.

Meditations

Chapter 1: Learning Peace Through Prayer

As you begin this time of practicing silence, offer the time itself to God. Tell Him that you are willing to have Him speak to you as He wants to speak, and that you are willing to hear what He says.

Take several moments to become *aware*, offering your whole self to God. What are your physical senses telling you? Thank God for your physical senses and for the magnificent instrument of your body.

What are you *doing?* Are you sitting still, or are you fidgeting? Are you comfortable or strained? Make sure you are in a position that will encourage alertness. Take several deep breaths, exhaling and inhaling deeply to encourage calmness.

What are you *thinking?* Are thoughts tumbling around in your head? Are you thinking about what you should be doing? Are problems controlling your thoughts? Offer your mind and its thought processes to God for this time of silence; ask Him to work creatively within the silence to bring about what He intends.

What are you *feeling?* Become aware of any emotions that might block God's speaking to you. Tell Him about your feelings and ask Him to remove any anger, fear, or guilt and replace the void with His love.

What are you *wanting?* What do you *really* want? Be honest with God and ask Him to bring your desires into harmony with His.

As you wait, do not be concerned about whether or not God will speak to you. Simply wait in the silence, being aware that God is with you, whether or not you can "feel" His presence.

Determine to spend this time listening instead of speaking. If you will keep up this discipline day by day, your ability to hear God's promptings will grow.

What do you think He wants to say to you? What gift does He have for you in these sacred times of drawing apart?

Read John 10:27, 28.

Chapter 2: Peace . . . and Love

After taking a few moments to "center," or settle down, picture yourself in a favorite place where you feel comfortable, safe, and at peace. Your favorite place may be a place in nature, a cathedral or church, or a room in your own home. It may be right where you are.

Take a few moments to see the place in detail. Look, with your mind's eye, at the colors and shapes around you. Slowly, carefully, let your eyes wander all over that holy space you have selected. Savor the feeling of peace that is there.

Listen to whatever sounds are in your imaginary space. If there are sounds in the actual space where you are, don't fight them. Simply accept them and allow them to be, for whatever we resist persists. If nagging thoughts or worries or items from your daily "to do" list pop into your mind, don't engage with them and don't resist them. Simply notice them and tell yourself you will deal with those things later. Then, gently bring your attention back to your imaginary place.

Take a few more deep breaths, letting go of any tension held in your body and relaxing more deeply. What aromas do you smell? What is the temperature of the place you are in? Is there any tension in your body? As you breathe, imagine that you are releasing any tension you are carrying.

When you feel centered and have the picture of your favorite imaginary place in your mind's eye, picture Jesus Christ walking toward you. Become aware of your feelings as the Prince of Peace, your Friend, walks toward you. Invite Him to sit down beside you. Tell Him how you feel, in your imagination, about His being there with you.

Imagine that you hear Christ telling you how much He loves you. Hear His tender voice speaking words of solace and comfort. Respond with whatever you want to tell Him.

Then, imagine that Christ tells you that He wants to transform your relationships. What person or persons pop into your mind? Note any feelings of anxiety or fear or anger. Tell Him exactly how you feel about that person and that relationship. Tell Him how you feel about being changed.

Listen, then, to what He wants to tell you. Ask Him to heal the broken parts of your own inner and, perhaps, warring selves. Hear Him again tell you how much He loves you.

After a period of silence, when you feel that you have heard all that Christ has to say for this time, record your impressions about this meditation time in your journal.

Read 1 John 4:7–11.

Chapter 3: The Third Party

After you have prepared for this time of encounter with the Living Christ, imagine that He is sitting with you in the favorite place of your imagination.

Turn your attention inward to discover what it is within you that is thwarting Christ's love from flowing through you to others.

Instead of thinking about what others might have done to you, open your mind and heart to the convicting presence of Christ, who wants to heal you of any self-defeating thoughts and beliefs and of harmful feelings and habits.

Project yourself out five years from now if you do not allow Christ to heal you of your self-defeating patterns. How will things be if you do not allow Him to change you with His love? What will you have lost? What if you hold on to your willfulness for ten more years? How will your life be if you stay locked in your present fear or anger for ten more years?

Acknowledge to the Living Christ who is with you that you cannot fix yourself. Tell Him that you would like to be changed from the inside out. If you are not willing for Him to do this, tell Him! Honesty clears the communication pathways between Christ and His friends.

If you are *willing* to be *made willing,* tell Him that. He takes us where we are and then does in us what we allow Him to do. In specific words, surrender as much as you can and know of yourself to as much as you know of God.

Tell Christ your fears about being changed. Ask Him for the clarity to see with His eyes. Accept His mercy and grace.

Read Proverbs 28:13, Isaiah 53:6, and 1 John 1:9.

Chapter 4: The Face in the Mirror

As you sit in your favorite place, ask the Living Christ to bring to your mind the most important people in your life, one by one.

As each of these significant others comes into your imagination, ask that person to sit down with you and the Peacemaker. Ask each one to tell you how he perceives your love for him. Ask each one to tell you what he needs from you and wants from you. Ask how that person would remember you if you were gone.

As each person talks to you in this imaginary conversation, do not respond. Do not justify yourself or argue with the person's comments. Be aware, however, of your feelings about what he is saying. Simply allow the person to speak his mind and receive the information with calmness and openness.

After each person has spoken in your imagination, turn your attention to the Living Christ and ask Him to tell you what He wants to about each relationship. It may be different from what the person tells you!

Acknowledge your inability, as a fallible human being, to love perfectly, and ask the Living Christ to grant you His love.

Read 1 Thessalonians 3:12 and make this your daily prayer.

Chapter 5: Boundaries for Freedom

In the quietness, turn to your Companion, the Living Christ. As you sit in the silence with Him, ask Him to reveal to you the people, places, events, roles, or things you have allowed to take first priority in your life. Let Him show you what has become master over you or what or whom you have allowed to become an idol in your life.

Ask Christ to place His finger on the people or things you have looked to to give you comfort or security.

Ask Christ to show you the people whose boundaries you have violated. These may be physical, emotional, intellectual, or spiritual boundaries that you have crossed, trying to control or, often out of good motivation, "protect" another human being.

What does Christ want to tell you about this problem? How would your life be different if you served only Christ as Master and allowed the other parts of your life to take their proper place?

What changes does Christ want to make in your life right now?

Read Luke 16:13.

Chapter 6: Instruments of His Peace

In your holy space, using the gift of your imagination, bring the awareness of the Living Christ's sitting with you to the "front" of your attention.

Allow your mind to take a tour through your weekly obligations and responsibilities. Think of the places you go and the people with whom you interact. See yourself involved in those places *with Christ's presence right beside you.* How does this change your actions and words?

Ask Christ to reveal to you how He wants you to be an instrument of His peace. Ask Him the things He wants you to do to make peace (which is different from "keeping peace"). Ask Him to tell you what to say. What changes do you need to make? Where do you need to put your boundaries in place? Where do you need to be more open and vulnerable? Where do you need to extend forgiveness or acceptance?

As Christ's Spirit reveals the truth to you about your relationships and your role as a peacemaker, record your insights in your journal. Remember that acting on the guidance Christ gives reveals more guidance, so make specific plans for carrying out what He asks you to do.

Read John 14:26, 27.

214

Chapter 7: Look to the Other Side

For this meditation, choose to create another imaginary space in which you will encounter the Living Christ. If you have been meeting Him indoors, go outside and find another place. If you have been seeing Him come to you in a place of nature, find another imaginary space inside of a building, either your home or a cathedral.

See yourself approaching Christ instead of Him approaching you. Become aware of how you feel as you walk toward Him. How does He greet you? What do you say to Him? What do you do?

Do you feel secure in approaching the Savior? Are you apprehensive? Do you go gladly or reluctantly, as a friend or a guilty child? Who starts the conversation?

As you sit in the silence, ask Christ to reveal to you what is out of balance in your own life. Ask Him to show you what problems this imbalance might be causing in your relationships. Ask Him to give you specific guidance in effecting change to bring about balance.

Read Romans 8:26.

Chapter 8: Power Transformed

In your meditation time, see yourself walking along a lakeside with a person you love. Visualize Christ joining you on your walk together.

Describe to Christ something about this person that you would like to change. Tell Him all the reasons it would be beneficial for the person to change. Tell Christ all the ways you have tried to change or "help" the person change.

Imagine that Christ listens patiently to your explanations.

Imagine that the other person listens, too, without reacting or justifying himself.

Now, tell "what else" you want Christ to know about your control of this beloved friend. Get everything out in the open.

What does Christ say to you about your efforts to change this other human being? What does He say to the other person?

You can also turn this meditation experience around and let the other person tell Christ, in your presence, how he feels about your attempts to change him, and then allow Christ to speak to both of you about the issue.

Another variation is for you to talk to the Living Christ about how it feels to be controlled by the other person, and then listen to His words of grace.

Read 1 Corinthians 13.

Chapter 9: Staying In

In your imagination, go back to the days of your first love, before you were married. Remember the excitement and the hope you felt, the eagerness for the future together that you and your husband or wife shared. Recall your wedding ceremony.

Now, in your meditation time, see yourself and your spouse sitting in a special place with the Living Christ, the Divine Third, between you. See Christ look first into your eyes, and then into the eyes of your spouse. Be aware of His love and tenderness.

Imagine what it would be like if each of you were to accept the forgiveness of Christ for all the ways you have harmed each other. Take a minute to talk about that with Him. Don't hesitate to talk about the resistance to forgive and the tendency to hold grudges.

Let Christ tell you what it does to your marriage to continue to stain it with grudges and resentments of past history. Let Him tell you, in your imagination, how it would be if you released each other from the judgments and criticisms that are choking His love from flowing through you.

As you sit there with your spouse in Christ's presence, accept the healing love Christ wants to give to each of you and to your marriage. Carry this picture with you into the tasks of the day.

Read Matthew 7:1–6.

Chapter 10: A Little Child Shall Lead Them

Return, in your imagination, to the place where you are most comfortable for your encounter with Christ. See yourself sitting with your child or with your own inner child.

How does your child respond to you? Does he want to be with you? Does he feel safe with you? Does he feel free to share his thoughts and feelings with you without fear of judgment?

Picture the Living Christ coming and sitting down between the two of you. Which one of you feels more at home with Him there between you? Which one of you speaks first in your imaginary encounter?

As the three of you sit quietly, hear the Living Christ ask the child to tell you what is on his mind and heart. See yourself receiving the information with openness and not with defensiveness. Tell the child that he is a gift from God to you and that you know that, in many ways, the child is your teacher.

Turn your attention to the Living Christ. How does He interpret the child's words to you? What does Christ confirm from the child's message?

217

Now, what would you like to say to the child, in the presence of Christ? How does the child receive your words?

What does the Living Christ say to the two of you?

Read Matthew 19:14.

Chapter 11: Partner on the Journey

As you enter into your time of silence, picture the Living Christ sitting down with you at a banquet table. As the two of you sit there in the fellowship and friendship that you have nurtured through your times of daily communion, be aware of the joy you sense in being in His presence. Be aware of what it is like to be totally accepted and loved and, therefore, to be completely comfortable in His presence. Take a few moments to savor and enjoy the serenity of being in the presence of Christ.

Hear Christ tell you that He has invited another guest, a human friend through whom He wants to mediate His love, grace, and mercy to each of you. Hear Him tell you how He wants to speak to each of you through the other and how He has taken the initiative to bring this person into your life as a soul friend.

Become aware that someone—another human instrument—is approaching you. Who is it? How do you feel about this soul friend whom Christ has brought into your life?

What does the person do? What do you say to the person?

More important than anything, what does Christ say to you about the friendship the two of you are to share?

Read Luke 24:13–31.

Chapter 12: The Healing Body

In your imagination, travel to a gathering of your church family, or of a church body that you might encounter. See yourself seated in the midst of this body of people. Hear the noises. See the faces of the people and the fixtures of the physical space.

Where do you sit in this group? Are you on the outside or the inside? Do you feel comfortable or awkward there? What do the others say to you, if anything? What do you say to them?

Picture the Living Christ walking into the room, with only you being able to recognize Him as Christ. What does He do? What person does He approach first? Whom does He touch with His healing, loving hands.

See Christ moving up and down the rows, whispering in the ears of some, directly confronting others. What difference does it make in the atmosphere when Christ is there? What difference does it make to you? Whom does He forgive? How do you feel about that?

Now, see yourself as the instrument of Christ, moving into your church family. If you are His spokesperson and the channel of His love, what will you do with that gift? If the Kingdom of God is truly within you, how will that change the way you relate to your fellow believers?

Read Romans 13:3–21.

Chapter 13: Here . . . and Beyond

After you have centered yourself in Christ's presence, see yourself walking out the door of your house. Using your typical mode of transportation, see yourself going up and down the streets of

219

your community. Visualize yourself going in and out of the businesses and restaurants of your community.

Hear yourself talking with the people you meet on a regular basis. When you carry out a transaction with a stranger, pause to look into that stranger's eyes, seeing beyond his role and moving beyond treating him as an object, to recognizing that he, like you, is a beloved child of God, created in the very image of God.

In the middle of your journey around your community, become aware that you are Christ's ambassador, a carrier of the Good News of the transforming grace of Christ. You are, for some, the representative of Christ on earth.

How does that awareness change your transactions? How does the knowledge that you are Christ's instrument affect the way you do business and confront the challenges and problems of everyday living? How does being Christ's instrument of peace change the way you talk? What does Christ's friendship with you do to your friendship with the world?

Read Ephesians 4:1–3.

Bibliography

Arapakis, Maria. *Softpower!* New York: Warner Books, Inc., 1990.

Beattie, Melody. *Co-Dependent No More.* Minneapolis: Hazelden Foundation, 1987.

Bonhoeffer, Dietrich. *Life Together.* New York: Harper and Row, 1954.

Carse, James P. *The Silence of God.* New York: Macmillan Publishing Company, 1985.

Chambers, Oswald. *My Utmost for His Highest.* New York: Dodd, Mead & Company, 1935.

de Waal, Esther. *Living With Contradiction.* San Francisco: Harper and Row Publishers, 1989.

Hendrix, Harville. *Getting the Love You Want.* New York: Henry Holt and Company, Inc., 1988.

Kelsey, Morton T. *Caring.* Ramsey, N.J.: Paulist Press, 1981.

Leech, Kenneth. *Soul Friend.* New York: Harper and Row, 1977.

L'Engle, Madeleine. *Two-Part Invention.* New York: Farrar, Straus and Giroux, 1988.

MacDonald, George. *Creation in Christ.* Wheaton, Ill.: Harold Shaw Publishers, 1976.

Mason, Mike. *The Mystery of Marriage.* Portland, Ore.: Multnomah Press, 1985.

Merton, Thomas. *New Seeds of Contemplation*. New York: New Dimensions Publishing Corporation, 1962.

Miley, Jeanie. *Creative Silence*. Dallas: Word Publishing, 1989.

Nouwen, Henri. *Reaching Out*. Garden City, N.Y.: Doubleday and Company, Inc., 1975.

————. *With Open Hands*. Notre Dame, Ind.: Ave Maria Press, 1972.

Paul, Jordan and Margaret. *Do I Have to Give Up Me to Be Loved by You?* Minneapolis: CompCare Publications, 1983.

Peck, Scott. *The Different Drum*. New York: Touchstone, by Simon and Schuster, 1987.

Schaef, Anne Wilson. *Escape From Intimacy*. San Francisco: Harper and Row, 1989.

Weatherhead, Leslie D. *The Transforming Friendship*. Nashville: Abingdon Press, 1977.